john timpson

HOW TO RIDE
A GIRAFFE

First published in 2008 by Caspian Publishing Ltd

198 Kings Road, London, SW3 5XP
T: +44 (0)20 7368 7100
F: +44 (0)20 7368 7201
www.caspianpublishing.co.uk

A catalogue record for this book is available from the British Library.

ISBN 978-1-901844-72-6

Designed by Jenny Knowles
Illustrations by Nicola Jennings
Printed and bound by TJ International Ltd, Padstow, Cornwall

CONTENTS

FOREWORD

Not many retail businesses last more than a lifetime. John Timpson's great-grandfather started his company in 1869. It is now an integral part of the British high street. Its success is something of which the Timpson family can be rightly proud.

As a retailer, there are qualities that shine through in this book, which gives you a clear and honest look at one of the UK's most distinctive family-owned companies.

I was struck by the company's ability to adapt and change over the decades. First it sold, then it made and now it repairs shoes. But it also cuts keys, makes house nameplates and repairs watches. It has been, temporarily, out of family control but now is firmly independent.

Another aspect of Timpson that really stands out is their unquenchable belief in individual initiative. Across the UK, Timpson employees are free to exercise their judgment to provide excellent customer service.

It is not just retail businesses that can learn from Timpson – every business can.

Miles Templeman
Director General, Institute of Directors

WHY *HOW TO RIDE A GIRAFFE*?

My first book, *Dear James*, had a title before I had written a word. With this book I reached the third and final draft and still didn't know what to call it. We tried a number of ideas: *A Voyage Round My Business*, *The Magic Dust* and *Controversial Common Sense* were all considered – and rejected.

Then I remembered an article about Timpson for which the journalist didn't just interview me but also met a cross-section of Timpson colleagues. This included Rod Umpleby, who was (until his retirement in 2004) our shopfitting and maintenance controller – a straight-talking Yorkshireman who watched the business grow from 150 to 550 shops and turnover increase from £12m to £100m.

"I think of the Timpson business as a giraffe," said Rod. "It has evolved and been shaped by events – no one could have possibly planned to produce a business like this, but it works."

At first I thought Rod's reference to a giraffe was rather odd. Then I realised that what appears to me quite normal is strange to the rest of the world. But there is no doubt that the Timpson giraffe has worked well. This book describes how we can keep it working. Hence, *How to Ride a Giraffe*.

ACKNOWLEDGEMENTS

I would like to thank all the people who took time to talk to me about our business, especially Paresh Majithia, Perry Watkins, Alex Barrett, Rosemary Whitehead, Karina Kenna, Darren Brown and Barbara Mead, whose initial interviews in Spring 2007 gave me the momentum to get on and write this book.

Christine Hickman, my PA, showed considerable patience in typing up several drafts of the manuscript, while Russ Sanders helped compile the illustrations. Michael McAvoy gave valuable guidance on the final draft before the editing was done by Stuart Rock, who then handed over a final draft to his team at Caspian, who in turn presented the finished product to the printer.

I would particularly like to thank my wife, Alex, who had the brilliant idea of buying our house in Rhoscolyn on Anglesey, for giving me permission to stay there in solitude for four weeks in August where I wrote the first draft. And finally, thanks to my son James, our managing director, who commissioned the project early in 2007 when he said to me, "it's time you wrote another book".

It is nice to still feel wanted.

DEDICATION

This book could not have been written without the help of the countless colleagues who have created a very successful business in a particularly difficult section of the high street.

Together we have discovered how to ride our giraffe.

Chapter 1
INTRODUCTION

In 1999, shortly before my son James became managing director, I wrote a book entitled *Dear James*. In it I passed on the lessons I had learned from my previous 39 years in business. Since then, things have turned out far better than I could possibly have imagined. I hope my book played its part, but James, perhaps revealing his mother's independent streak, has never relied totally on my advice. He often seeks inspiration from elsewhere. In 2006 he went to the US on a trip organised by the consultancy, ?What If! He visited South West Airlines, W L Gore, MGM and Ritz Carlton in the company of 25 upwardly mobile senior managers. It was an expensive trip, so it had to be good. But I was worried. I feared James would return with loads of radical ideas that would signal the end of my time in charge of Timpson strategy.

My fears were unfounded. James came back full of enthusiasm but with no hint of a U-turn. He rang me straight after stepping off the plane. "We already do most of the things they do," he said. "They have the same values and operate by the same principles. If they have it right, we have too. I don't want to change anything. But we do have a problem," he added, and a more serious edge crept into his voice. What was he going to say? "We don't realise why our business has become so successful. So far, we've got where we are almost by chance. We have introduced lots of ideas that work, so we now need to understand what those ideas are. We have to identify what has created our success."

James and I live so close to the business that we probably don't realise how different it has become. Few companies give such freedom to employees and have so few rules. (How many other multiple retailers allow their shop staff to treat the price list purely as a guide?) It is a business based on trust – we give our staff authority to run the business. Head Office is not allowed to issue orders and computers can't take control. There are few formal meetings and no memos. Instead, we have our own weekly 16-page newsletter that is mainly about our people.

We call our style "upside-down management." It is based on the simple premise that the people who serve our customers run the business and that everyone else is there to help them do it. It was brought in to improve personal service. We have always seen good customer care as a major competitive opportunity.

Retailing has become a numbers game. Using market research and information from barcodes, head offices decide the strategy and orders are issued by tough line managers. In some shops, even the customers must follow the rules. A rigid formula creates control and consistency, but it doesn't allow branch staff to give their customers the individual attention that is the hallmark of great customer care.

In this numbers-driven world, people become payroll statistics. They are part of the wage costs shown in the monthly management accounts. Most managers say that "people are our biggest asset". But do they really believe it?

Our business success almost entirely depends on people. We provide a service, so our quality depends on the skill level of colleagues who work in our branches. We spend a lot on training as it is the best way to improve our business. Yet training only works with good people. For upside-down management to succeed, a talented middle-management team has to "get it". Middle management in our upside-down management world is a special skill. We spend lots of time and money on management training to help them develop their team.

It is vital to look after both superstars and loyal employees. They create our success. Our long list of employee benefits includes holiday homes, a final salary pension scheme, football tickets and a hardship fund. Everyone gets their birthday off. We really do try to be a great place to work.

Some people think it odd that we have prospered without the help of professional management. We are a family business owned by the family and run by the family. We don't have to bother about market analysts or institutional shareholders. We are fiercely independent and do things our way. We have been called quirky and maverick, but despite ignoring standard management practice we have been pretty successful. In the 12 years from 1995 to 2007, our 200 shops increased to 570. Turnover increased from £30m to £100m, and profits rose from £700,000 to £12.5m; instead of borrowings, we have money in the bank.

We operate in an unfashionable sector – few people seek their fortune in shoe repairs and key cutting – and it is not an area where many have made serious money. Our two major competitors both made losses. Eventually we bought one from the receiver and the other for £1, making us the UK's market leader in all the main services we provide.

Perhaps our particular management style works because our trade is so different. We are the only significant blue-collar service shop on the high street. We are the ultimate "people business". Our success totally depends on our people, particularly those who serve our customers. That thought has driven everything we do. We developed upside-down management because it is what our business needs. I wouldn't want to run it any other way. We have the confidence to do things differently because we know our business so well. James and I spend at least two days every week out of the office visiting the shops. We know them in detail – we both visit them all every 18 months – and we meet most of the people who work for us. But, as James pointed out to me, we are possibly too close to the business to identify the vital ingredients that created our success.

I read recently a piece of research from the London School of Economics that concluded – and here I summarise – the best way to ruin a good business is to hand it over to the eldest son. What a load of rubbish. Much of our recent success is due to James's energy and enthusiasm. I hope we have proved that a father-and-son team can provide the perfect combination of vitality and experience. James has come up with many of the ideas we have introduced over the past five years and, as managing director, he has implemented all of them. Neither of us can imagine doing a more satisfying job. Our *Mastermind* subject is "Shoe Repair Shops of Great Britain" – and these days James would win. Nowadays I struggle to keep up. With youth on his side, James has the stamina to travel more miles and pack more into a week.

Recently we visited our store in St Albans. It is one of our oldest shops and also one we have visited the most. (After he got married, James lived nearby and often popped in to serve customers there.) On this occasion it was being run by one of our mobile managers, Sean Smith.

"How do you think you will do today?" asked James.

"With a bit of luck, I will get to £600," said Sean.

"That would be amazing," said James (St Albans' average take is £400 a day). "Tell you what. If you make £600, give me a call on my mobile."

At 5.15pm an excited Sean rang. "I've taken £730," he said.

"That's fantastic," replied James. "Book yourself a meal, go out with your partner, have a really good evening and send me the bill."

The way James and I work together is a mini version of upside-down management. He runs the business and I'm there to help. Sometimes he asks me to do a few tasks – like writing this book.

"Talk to the people who know our business even better than we do," James said to me. "Talk to colleagues who have helped this business flourish. These are the people who care about the company and want to see it go from strength to strength." So that is what I did. I met a number of Timpson superstars and asked them what mattered most. Their comments have dictated the contents of this book. I am grateful to them for telling me so much about the company I love.

Chapter 2
OUR HISTORY

Our business has been formed by many chance incidents and accidents. My great-grandfather, who founded the original Timpson shoe business in 1869, would be amazed to discover that his company has become a cobbler, key cutter, engraver and watch repairer.

Great-grandpa started as a shop assistant, working in his uncle's shoe shop in Butler Street, Manchester. He was only 16 but before long he went into business on his own in Oldham Street, near the city centre. He lived above the shop, married and brought up 12 children and still found plenty of time to develop his business. After a few years he started opening shops in the Manchester suburbs.

In 1903 he added shoe repairs, using a central factory in Hulme. It was a three-day service, with a horse and cart moving customers' shoes between shop and factory. Shoe repairing was very different in those days. A shoe repair factory was exactly that: it was a production line with operatives specialising in each part of the shoe repair job – preparation, benching and finishing – supported by apprentices who moved the stock and tidied up. Forty people worked in the original factory.

Most new retailers struggle to grow beyond 15 shops. Great-grandpa didn't have that problem; after all, he had 12 children to help. By 1920 he had 50 branches with shops in Sheffield, Liverpool and Edinburgh.

Most new shops were too far away to use his shoe repair factory in Manchester, so other new workshops were established in the low-rent suburbs. In 1929, the year that great-grandpa died, a factory opened in Liverpool above an empty shop that my grandfather then turned into a collection depot. It was our first proper shoe repair shop.

GETTING SERIOUS ABOUT SHOE REPAIRS

In 1939 Timpson had 200 shoe shops and 15 separate repair branches. By 1950 shoe repair had become a serious Timpson business and a separate organisation was established – the Footwear Repairs Division (FRD).

This new subsidiary grew rapidly and took advantage of the changing nature of the Timpson shop portfolio. Many of the suburban shoe shops had fairly basic living accommodation above them (I saw several while visiting branches with my father when I was a teenager). Despite our attempts to keep the flats in a reasonable state of repair, gradually managers moved away and the rooms became vacant. So the FRD put repair factories upstairs into more than 100 shoe shops. They subsequently added a separate repair counter in the actual shop with their own dedicated counter girls (men worked in the factory!). This started a deep-seated rivalry between shoe shop staff and the repair business. Shoe shop managers resented the counter girls who charged different prices for shoe care products and ignored customers waiting to buy shoes.

These "in shop" factories provided a much quicker service. Instead of three days, they could provide a next-day or even a same-day service. This meant less work for the big central factories on which the business had been built. Gradually they were closed.

The arrogant and aggressive FRD found another development route. In the 1950s several old Timpson branches were considered too suburban or out of position for shoe retail and were converted to specialist shoe repair shops. Many were in low-income areas where we would struggle today, but in 1950 the economics of shoe repairing were very different. Secondary shopping locations in Ellesmere Port and Patricroft don't appear exciting today, but FRD made them successful. They were encouraged to open sites from scratch in small suburbs around Manchester, such as Northenden, Longsight and Handforth. They also opened a few city-centre shops in Coventry, St Albans, as well as our oldest surviving shop – Wilmslow – which opened in 1956.

My father taught me that if you can repair shoes for less than one-third of the price of a new pair, you're in business. That rule is still true today, but he would be surprised to see how many more shoes we now repair in the winter. In the 1950s winter was our quiet time because, in the days before central heating and universal car driving, from November onwards most people wore winter boots that didn't need repairing.

Shoes in the 1950s were very different. Everyone wore leather. Everyone used a cobbler. Shoes were relatively expensive, so even the cheapest were worth repairing. The shoe repair market was ten times bigger than today and was about to get even bigger.

The fashion cycle headed back to pointed toes – and this time they were winkle pickers with stiletto heels. The FRD could not have expanded at a better time. The new four-hour service was ideal for heels. Eventually shoe repairs became a while-you-wait business. We started to see heel bars repairing stilettos with barefoot customers sitting on stools waiting for the job to be completed.

Winkle picker court shoes helped to create a new Timpson service – shoe dyeing. Customers paid a high price for our 24-hour recolouring service and we enjoyed extremely generous margins.

As a sign of its importance, the Footwear Repair Department changed its name to Timpson Shoe Repairs (TSR). Everything TSR touched turned to gold. Yet in 1963 it was heading for disaster – and nobody realised.

RECESSION HITS SHOE REPAIRS

The decline in stilettos was probably predictable, as fashion moves consistently through a 20-year cycle. Wide toes and thick heels replaced the winkle pickers and stilettos. Fewer customers came to TSR.

What was less expected was the dramatic change in shoe construction. This was first seen with the launch of Tuf shoes for men, with their cheap leather uppers, moulded rubber soles and a six-month guarantee. This new brand had a big influence on the men's shoe market. A substantial percentage of manufacturers replaced traditional leather with the new hard-wearing soles.

There were also major changes in women's shoes, as leather uppers and soles were replaced by harder-wearing synthetics. Up until then, 90 per cent of the shoes in our shops were made in Britain. In the 1960s imports increased dramatically and the real price of new shoes came tumbling down. Faced with cheaper footwear and less stilettos, shoe repairers were plunged into crisis. Sales fell by 15 per cent for three years running. By 1969 half of our shoe repair business had disappeared. To rub salt in the wound, the lucrative dyeing business was suspended because its toxic chemicals were made illegal.

We closed a number of unprofitable units but concentrating turnover into fewer shops wasn't enough. Something more dramatic had to be done. In a desperate bid to increase sales, shoe repair shops introduced merchandise. They had always sold shoe care products but the big new idea was to sell something else. Competitors such as Paynes and Coombes started to sell leather goods – so did we. We sold "portable leather goods" (such as purses and wallets) and briefcases. We were big into shopping bags, particularly straw bags and tote bags. We even sold cheap footwear, including sandals and slippers.

The success story was hosiery, particularly when tights were introduced in 1967 to go with hot pants and the mini skirt. Most shops had a wall full of hosiery and took big money (sadly at a low margin, but they brought in lots of regular customers). Merchandise was the responsibility of our counter girls who ran the retail part of the business. The factory was either upstairs, in the basement or out at the back and was staffed by men with specialist roles. (The three main job titles were benchman, finisher and boy.) This team never saw a customer; even the branch manager spent most of his time in the factory.

The bonus scheme, which is such an important part of Timpson operation today, started as a piece-rate system with factory operatives earning a small bonus for every job they did. The counter girl's bonus was based on beating a turnover target calculated by multiplying her wage cost by a magic number (merchandise sales were only worth half of shoe repair turnover for bonus purposes). The counter bonus worked so well that the piece work system was replaced by a new productivity bonus, with that target set by a multiple of the productive wages. It was a complicated system that worked well. Over the past 40 years it has been steadily simplified to produce today's branch bonus.

With sales dropping, wage control was the key to making money. Staff levels were reduced. In 1960 a branch might have employed four counter girls and eight operatives; in 1965 the same branch only had two counter girls and three operatives.

WHILE YOU WAIT

In the late 1960s a major shoe repair revolution brought a dramatic reduction in our wage bill. Heel bars were opening with stools in front of the counter and the repair work was being done behind a glass screen so customers could see their shoes being repaired. This inspired Dutch machinery manufacturers to develop an industry-changing idea. They organised all the equipment needed to repair shoes into a layout that could fit in the shop itself. It created today's shoe repair shop and was the difference between disaster and survival. The first Timpson conversion was in Newport Street in Bolton. The result was dramatic. Customers could see what was happening to their shoes and they liked watching people at work. The new layout encouraged same-day repairs. We realised the way to hang on to customers and beat the competition was to promote while-you-wait.

Initially, the benchmen and finishers felt awkward in the public gaze, however they had their backs to the customers and left service to the counter girls. But the advantage of shoe repairers talking to customers was evident. Shoppers liked being served by someone who knew what they were talking about and, if the operative served the customer, there was no longer the need for a counter girl.

Before long, the standard staff line-up for a new Timpson branch was manager, benchman, counter girl and boy. The wage bill dropped by 30 per cent and this gave us the chance to survive.

When merchandise was established as a permanent feature, buying became a serious job. Every shop had shoe care products, hosiery, portable leather goods, baskets, tote bags and gifts. A military-style weekly display guide stopped most shops looking like an Aladdin's cave.

For the next few years shoe repair sales continued to decline. Our merchandise turnover, although welcome, didn't bring enough extra margin to compensate. Something else was needed.

We experimented with all sorts of activities. We tried knife sharpening. We sold cassette tapes. We repaired spectacles. We tried to take in dry cleaning. The one thing that started to take in money was key cutting. Demand for keys was going up at the same time as traditional ironmongers were disappearing from the high street. It was also one of the few services that customers could receive as an impulse purchase. This was why cobblers started to cut keys.

LIFE WITH UDS

Our first shop to provide a key-cutting service was Tib Street in Manchester (close to where great-grandpa started the business).

Initially the concept struggled. The benchmen said that the new equipment got in the way. The counter girls were only deemed strong enough to cut cylinder keys (the versions often referred to as Yale keys). Mortice keys (the Chubb-type latch keys) were seldom cut by anyone.

We developed an L-shape at the end of the counter to accommodate keys and to stop the benchmen whingeing. But in 1973 the average branch had a key-cutting turnover of still only £10 per week.

Then we had a stroke of luck. The Timpson business had just become part of the UDS group [see chapter 3]. The group included Richard Shops, a ladies fashion chain that was enjoying great success from a new, simple-angled display in its windows. TSR converted the Richard shop fixture to display keys and put it right in front of the window of four branches. Sales doubled. Before long, the trial branches were taking £50 a week. The display was introduced into every shop. We had the makings of a key business. With merchandise performing well and a new-found enthusiasm for keys, TSR was back in profit and looking forward to the return of slim heels in the 1980s.

The acquisition of Timpson by UDS in 1973 was good for TSR. The UDS management liked the cash TSR created and admired its management style. They left everything to the fiercely independent group that ran it – Michael Frank, Alan Chatterton and Charles Noakes.

During the late 1970s TSR started a campaign to provide better customer service and began to break away from the traditional image of the dirty, grumpy cobbler. In 1979 it was stipulated that everyone had to wear a tie; it was a symbol that TSR had finally turned into a retailer.

OUR FIRST ACQUISITION

Gradually TSR moved out of the Timpson shoe shops. More stand-alone repair shops were opened, providing key-cutting and the full range of merchandise. With 160 branches by 1979, TSR was the second-largest player in the UK market. The biggest, Allied Shoe Repairs, had steadily acquired many chains such as Coombes, Malones and Shoecraft.

UDS was keen to see TSR grow and identified two takeover targets. The first was the Luton-based WH Broughall chain, with 35 shops. I met the Broughall family with Stuart Lyons, the managing director of UDS, for a pub lunch in Dunstable. Their business was struggling and we bought it for a modest £275,000. Only seven out of the 35 shops still trade, but last year they contributed £504,000. Not a bad deal!

We were also keen to buy Shoecare, a business based in Kent. Its owner, Brian Smith, had 12 shops plus a factory making moccasins in Aylesford. I negotiated a price of £175,000 with him but the UDS finance director told me to do better. Negotiations were put on hold for nine months until the UDS managing director stepped in. He agreed to pay Brian £225,000 plus a £15,000 index-linked annuity. When Brian died in 2006 the annuity was providing £57,000 a year and the total he had received for the business had reached £967,000. Only five of those shops are still trading. They made a £175,000 contribution last year, so it was a reasonable return on our investment but I know which was the better deal. It was a very expensive lesson about the cost of an annuity.

In 1983 the ownership of the company changed twice. Initially, UDS was acquired by the conglomerate Hanson Trust; later in the year I led a management buyout. Timpson was back in private hands and we had control of our destiny.

TOUGH TIMES IN THE EIGHTIES

Despite the return of slim heels in the 1980s, toes were not nearly as narrow as the winkle pickers of the 1960s and heels were not as slim. The turnover increase created by the fashion cycle did not compensate for a new threat – trainers. In five years, 25 per cent of the shoe market had switched to footwear that was never repaired. At the same time, imports forced the price of new shoes down. Shoe repairers were under more pressure than ever before. We were particularly hard hit in the Northern towns and suburbs where our core business was based. Shoe repair was becoming a service for wealthy customers. Shoes were so cheap that we could not meet my father's "one-third" rule. However, a new competitor – Automagic – was doing well in London, Milton Keynes and Croydon while we were suffering in Jarrow and Moss Side. We closed 30 shops. It was essential cost-cutting but not a long-term solution.

The lifeline came out of the blue. Desperate to find a way to arrest our decline in sales and profit, I had a brainstorm meeting with Kit Green, who was shortly to succeed Mike Frank as managing director. We came up with a wild idea. Realising services provided a much better margin than merchandise, we picked two shops – Leicester and Gloucester – and replaced a complete wall of merchandise with an enormous board full of keys. Immediately key turnover doubled; the extra margin more than compensated for the replacement of bags and shopping baskets. We tried ten more shops – with the same result. Within three years, every shop had a big keyboard and we were making money.

Originally, we saw the big keyboard as a marketing ploy. But it changed the whole business. Customers now saw us as expert key cutters. Even the most reluctant benchman started to take key cutting seriously.

In 1985 we heard our competitor Allied Shoe Repairs (ASR) was up for sale. As all our efforts were concentrated on our shoe shops, we didn't have a strategy for shoe repairs. We had no idea what Allied was worth. Despite this, my non-executive directors persuaded me to offer £10m. I met Fergus Watson, the chairman of ASR, for lunch in London. He confirmed that ASR had decided to sell its shoe repair subsidiary. I made the offer and he promised to get back to me. Two weeks later he rang to tell me he had sold the business to another major competitor, Mr Minit. They probably paid £10.5m.

TIMPSON SHOE REPAIRS BECOMES INDEPENDENT

By January 1987, TSR profits had improved but within months there would be another major change. In May, we sold the shoe shops to Olivers [see page 33]. By Christmas, TSR was an entirely separate business, run from its new office and warehouse in Claverton Road, Wythenshawe. Most people thought I had little interest in shoe repairs. I had, after all, spent most of my life in shoe retailing. It was rumoured that I would soon sell TSR. Mike Strom, the chief executive of Automagic, certainly thought so. He rang me to talk about a deal.

After a tough few years I wanted an easy life. I had no plans to grow TSR beyond its existing size. I was happy with annual profits of £400,000 but soon realised that people in the business needed a clear signal that I was still up for it. The answer was to buy another business.

We negotiated with John Stratford and Chris Fowler to acquire Shoetech, a modern heel bar business with 12 good sites. I didn't have the money – so we gave them 18 per cent of our shares in a deal concluded two weeks before the stock market crash in September 1987.

We had agreed to float our business within three years. In 1989 I met stockbrokers to prepare a prospectus. Profits had doubled to £800,000 and I was advised a flotation would be successful. Then my wife Alex stepped in. "You would be mad," she said. "You could never work with institutional shareholders breathing down your neck. Stay on your own." I took her advice and bought out the Shoetech shareholders at a cost of £1.2m. It was a high price for 12 shops but 11 still trade today, contributing £750,000 per year. That was another good deal!

Shoetech taught us how to sell the extra job and created a dramatic increase in our sale of stick-a-soles. We plucked ace salesman Arthur Voller out of Shoetech to show us how he did it. We brought in a special offer – "heels free if sole done now". We already sold lots of extra keys (a "two keys for £1" offer that has evolved into our "second key half price"). Today, extra jobs bring £10m and provide half of our profits.

MAKING MORE ACQUISITIONS

By 1988 the big keyboard was making a real difference. We started engraving in 1969. (Having seen the benefit of a second service, we were literally scratching around for something else.) We installed a £2,000 pantograph in every shop but our total weekly nationwide engraving turnover was not getting beyond £3,000, being mainly pet tags and nurses' badges.

Then a sports retailer went bust in Tonbridge. Its shop was sub-let from the Shoetech branch next door. We decided to use it for specialist computerised engraving but the engraving machine took up too much space and required a dust-free environment. The computer went upstairs and, instead of doing dog tags and nurses' badges, started to produce house signs. It offered the service to other Timpson shops.

This was the real start of our engraving business. We bought another computer engraver and put it above our shop in St Helens. The service provided by the Tonbridge team left much to be desired. Most shops sent their work to St Helens, so we concentrated all the work there and moved out to an industrial park. Then we put computer engravers into some shops, starting in Solihull. Within weeks we could see the potential. Our weekly engraving turnover is now £180,000.

We had found how to grow our business despite the fall in shoe repairs: develop new services and buy the competition. Following the success of the Shoetech acquisition, we did two smaller but very profitable deals, British Shoe Corporation (BSC) Repairs and Lillywhites.

BSC had 35 concessions trading under the name The Menders within its shoe shops, along with some in department stores such as Selfridges. We paid £175,000 for the business and its first year contribution was £275,000. Today only one shop is left. But the survivor is the concession in Selfridges – which has been our top turnover shop every year since we bought it.

The purchase of 11 Lillywhite shops took us in a different direction. They were all concessions inside Johnson the Cleaners. This was our first link with Johnsons, where we now have 35 concessions.

We then purchased 12 shops around London from competitor Keith Dann; the seven shops that still trade today justify the high £1m price.

These acquisitions made a big difference. We grew to 220 branches and profits reached £1.6m in 1990. But they were only to sink back to £650,000 by 1994 as shoe repairing continued to decline.

DEVELOPING TALENT

The new shops didn't just produce extra turnover. They brought us new talent. Jim Malcolm (who has recently managed Rugby, Milton Keynes and Selfridges) was working for BSC in Corby. Our security manager Paul Myatt worked in Shoetech in Reading. Kerry Burke, our recently retired regional training manager, worked for Lillywhites in Rochdale where Ray Cooley, now a Timpson area development manager, was his area manager. Many people who joined us through acquisition have gone on to shape the future of our company.

As part of our plan to improve profits and deal with poorly performing shops, we franchised 35 branches. Initially it worked well, but we soon learned that success depended on the franchisee. Poor franchisees had to be baled out; those that did well wanted more out of life and looked for a bigger role. Although franchising only lasted seven years, we discovered some great talent in the process. Alan Madden in Motherwell, Alex Barrett in Kilmarnock, Ricky Bickell in Harlow, Graham Young in Harpenden, Winston Harris in Loughton, Bill O'Dell in Cheltenham and Chris Edwards in Gloucester were all successful franchisees who still do a great job for the company. When we inherited 35 Mr Minit franchises in 2003, they were quickly converted into Timpson-owned shops.

As shoe repairs continued to decline, our future depended on key cutting. We appointed a key-cutting product manager, Jim Jardine, who was previously area manager in the north-east. Having a key specialist made a difference as sales increased by 25 per cent a year. We then appointed key development managers (KDMs) in every area. This worked so well we appointed specialists to develop engraving and watch repairs.

The original KDMs were the predecessor of today's area development managers who, with the addition of mobile managers, provide comprehensive support for our branches. Most businesses would not make such a large investment in field overheads but we think differently. The introduction of key development managers helped to create the most important part of our management structure.

THE IMPORTANCE OF KEY CUTTING

Every idea connected with keys seemed to work. Many were designed to beat the car manufacturers, which tried to create keys that we could not cut. The Ford Tibbi key, for example, could only be copied by a main dealer. After spending two years and £75,000, we found a machine that cuts Tibbi keys to perfection. It brought so much extra business that we were encouraged to invest in technology that duplicated car alarm remotes and immobiliser keys. It got too technical for me, but I understood the profit key cutting brings.

Shoe repairers took keys to their heart. They enjoyed the job and wanted to learn more. Our locksmith courses were a great success: we taught them how to make a new key, change a lock, pick a lock and break into a car.

By the mid-1990s, we had established our key-cutting credentials; we were the only high street shop that aimed to cut every key every time. Ian Oakes, previously branch manager in Northwich, set up a helpline at Timpson House to answer queries and supply special blanks. The popularity of this key centre surprised me; the number of weekly calls grew rapidly to 2,000.

We stocked over 2,000 blanks. The comprehensive coverage of our keys was emphasised by our big keyboards. We changed the keyboard design every three years, from blue to yellow to red to vertical stripes and even to a triangular design. With every change, sales went up.

We needed the extra key business. In 1993 and 1994 shoe repair sales fell 20 per cent. It was difficult to maintain morale. I remember presenting a road show during a heat wave, with shoe repairs falling 25 per cent and overall sales down 12 per cent. The shop staff wanted to cut prices. The accountants wanted to cut costs. But I did nothing. When I visited the branches, I saw the same people running them as well as ever, but everyone was wearing sandals and flip flops and no one wanted shoe repairs.

Later I discovered we were doing much better than our competitors. Our profits in 1995 were less than £500,000, but Automagic produced two profit warnings and were about to announce a loss.

AUTOMAGIC: A MAJOR ACQUISITION

In the late 1980s and early 1990s I had several conversations with Mike Strom, the chairman of Automagic and its main shareholder. These were vague talks about a merger; to me, they were about Timpson buying Automagic, but to Mike Strom it was about Automagic buying Timpson. In 1992 we made a foolish move that stopped the talking. We bought 27 per cent of the Automagic shares from a Scottish investment company for £1m. We thought this would bring Mike Strom to the negotiating table; it had the reverse effect as he never spoke to me again.

But during the early 1990s we kept talking to Automagic's operations director Mike Kerly and its non-executive director John Talbot. In 1994 we nearly bought 20 shops, but we tried to chip the price and the deal fell through. A year later the Automagic losses got bigger and, under pressure from its bank, it agreed to sell us 30 branches.

We briefed the area managers on the day before this deal was to be signed and then I left for a family holiday in Wales. I was only there for four hours before the deal was off. Automagic had gone into receivership and we had missed the chance to buy 30 shops. I also lost £1m on the shares.

We had three weeks to decide how much to offer the receiver. Even after mortgaging our house for £1m and borrowing as much as the bank would allow, we were likely to be outgunned by our principal competitor, Mr Minit. But a miracle happened. After an all-night battle, we won the auction and Automagic was ours. We had jumped from 210 to 320 shops. All we had to do was turn their loss-making business into profit.

For four months Automagic continued to trade down on last year. But then three things made a difference. We put a big keyboard into every branch; it was temporary and cheap but it worked. Overnight we doubled the key business and overall sales went up by 20 per cent. Then we won the battle of London. Automagic had 14 well-situated inner London shops that lost money because the staff pinched significant sums from the till. Automagic London was effectively run by a mafia. Anyone who didn't steal was bullied and hounded out of the company. We set up a hit team to run each branch one by one and prove how much money could be taken. Gradually the criminals left and turnover went up. Today, thanks to our area manager, Chris Wellings, and his team, London branches take up to four times as much as they did with Automagic.

After six months we started a refit programme. When our new employees from Automagic saw this investment we gained their confidence. The business has never looked back. All of those 110 shops still trade profitably today. Currently 15 out of our 20 most profitable shops come from Automagic. The deal cost £4m, but last year ex-Automagic branches produced a contribution of £6m. It was probably the best deal we have ever done.

GETTING SERIOUS ABOUT TRAINING

We started to think seriously about training. I asked Mike Donoghue, then product manager for shoe repairs, how we set quality standards. "We aim to produce a good commercial job," he replied, "but we don't go into detail." That conversation prompted our first training manual, which was written in pictures with very few words. These manuals changed the profile of training, and training manager Peter Harris seized the opportunity with enthusiasm. In 1997 we introduced skill levels and skill tests to monitor standards and we linked skill levels to our bonus scheme. Connecting training with pay made a big difference. Something new has been added to Timpson training every year since 1996. In ten years we have spent over £25m on training – a large figure that has made a big difference.

Automagic brought us some great sites, particularly in London, and lots of good people such as regional manager Tony Sharpe; area managers Geoff Goodfellow and Les Hart; star shop managers Chris Hart in Brent Cross and Carmel Quirk in Moorgate; and many others. It also prompted our move into watch repairs.

THE START OF WATCH REPAIRS

Automagic had offered a watch repair service in Luton and Stevenage in conjunction with watch repairer John Lyons. A few weeks after our purchase of Automagic, I was in West Bromwich where manager Glenn Edwards was an experienced watch repairer. He asked whether he could offer a watch repair service in his shop. Encouraged by his initiative, we tested a watch strap and battery service in Fish Street Hill in the City of London, Crawley, Salisbury and Yeovil. We averaged a weekly £70 and were very pleased. At about this time, H Samuel came to Timpson House with a proposed joint venture about engraving. "But," said their sales manager, "we won't work with you if you continue to develop the watch repair service we have seen in Yeovil. Our watch repair turnover is £13.5m a year." That was all I needed to know!

James, who was then our marketing controller, booked watch repair training courses at the Horological Institute near Newark for four months. Nearly everyone one from Timpson learned the craft through expert watch repairer Vincent Light. In the summer of 1999 we had a big breakthrough. A major refit at Eastbourne included a separate watch repair kiosk at the front of the shop; it took £1,000 in the first week. We started to take watch repairs very seriously.

Glenn Edwards set up a central watch workshop in Wolverhampton and we became proper watch repairers. By 2003 watch repairs reached ten per cent of Timpson's total turnover.

In 1997 Mr Minit Worldwide was bought by the Swiss bank UBS. We had meetings with its previous owner, Don Hilsden-Ryan, but he never saw us as serious bidders for his UK business. So shortly after this deal I went to see Ian Siddall, who was in charge of Minit, to propose buying the UK business. My offer was arrogantly declined. "We are experts in buying family businesses and putting in professional management," he said. "You could be the next on my list."

This was serious competition. UBS had vast sums of money. We decided to compete by giving customers a good quality job and the best possible service. Our success, therefore, depended on how branch colleagues dealt with customers. I decided the way to provide that great personal service was to give branch staff total authority and to trust them to get on with it. It was this thought that led to the concept of upside-down management [see chapter 10].

UPSIDE-DOWN MANAGEMENT

I talked to our managing director Kit Green about it. In his usual laid-back way, he told me to give it a go. I wrote about upside-down management with great enthusiasm, describing the advantages of colleagues having the authority to use their initiative. Nothing changed. No one would believe that any business would have the courage to give its employees so much freedom.

I needed to do something dramatic. We introduced real-life examples of this new freedom. We announced that shop staff were to have individual authority to spend up to £500 to settle a complaint; we told them to treat our price list purely as a guide so that they could decide what price to charge. The message started to get across.

Upside-down management needed the support of our area managers, but they were reluctant to delegate. Every area had two or three area development managers (ADMs) who were often used as relief branch managers. Rather than fulfilling management roles, they spent their lives running a branch.

Area managers were frightened of delegating. "We are responsible for the results," they said. "If we give everyone freedom, we can't control what they do." They also feared that if the ADMs had a meaningful role there would be little left for the area manager to do.

It took three years of conferences, area visits and consistent determination before upside-down management started to work. To most people it is an odd way to run a business. For the past few years we have been pulling against a strong elastic which constantly tries to draw us back to traditional management techniques, but steadily our culture is getting stronger and the elastic much weaker.

ACQUIRING MR MINIT

In the late 1990s, with no prospect of buying Minit UK, we looked at other acquisitions. These included InTime, a watch repair concession inside Debenhams, and Sketchley, which also owned SupaSnaps. Talking didn't lead to a deal.

In 1999 both of these businesses were bought by Mr Minit. Ian Siddall had plans to create a global business based on a multi-service shop concept under the Minit Solutions brand. Several million pounds were spent on rebranding, retraining and refitting branches but with little success. In the summer of 2000 we offered to buy their UK shops. In the spring of 2001 we agreed to purchase 30 small Minit branches in the north of England but the deal fell through. (I received a fax while on holiday in the Caribbean saying Minit had changed its mind.)

Several people had a go at running Minit and we approached each managing director as he appeared on the scene. Eventually one Minit man took us seriously. Company doctor Howard Dyer had been brought in to save the company from serious trouble. After six months we had agreed a price of £1 for 700 shops. It was hardly a bargain as the shops had lost £120m in four years.

In April 2003 the purchase of Minit UK (including Sketchley and SupaSnaps) completely changed Timpson. It also brought a whole load of problems. SupaSnaps was declining fast in the face of digital photography and cameraphones. The 120 Sketchley branches were a demoralised bunch and most of their 111 concessions in Sainsbury's were based on the misconceived Minit Solutions format. After six months we decided to sell both SupaSnaps and Sketchley. It took a year to find a buyer. Klick bought SupaSnaps for £100,000 and we sold Sketchley to Johnson for £1. A large number of the Sainsbury's concessions were acquired by a new business being developed by Persil.

With the Minit branches, we had to decide what to do with the luggage, which produced 30 per cent of its turnover. The decision took us less than a month. As each Minit shop was refitted, luggage disappeared. Turnover and profit margins improved and, within two years, a business that had been losing £2m was producing a £3m profit.

RECENT MOVES

Once Sketchley and SupaSnaps had been sold and the conversion of Minit Shops to Timpson completed, our overdraft steadily reduced towards zero and we returned to more tranquil times. But the business has not stood still.

Between 2004 and 2007, we opened 60 new branches, including the acquisition of the 14-shop Uppermost chain in Scotland, trading under the name of Master Cobbler. In 2004 we acquired the House Nameplate Company (HNP), a major house sign supplier to B&Q and Homebase. A separate subsidiary, Keys Direct, supplies lockers and a key management system to multi-site employers such as Asda and Waitrose.

In 2006 we made a major commitment to our fast-growing locksmith business. This now aims to become the national UK locksmith service, with everything run on Timpson principles. I am too superstitious to forecast the future but, from what I have seen, our locksmith project deserves to succeed.

These new businesses give us more scope for future growth, but the core Timpson service chain earns the lion's share of our profit. And here, too, there have been developments such as the introduction of jewellery repairs and photo ID.

We were already committed to open 30 shops in 2008 when we bought Persil Services – a further 40-plus concessions in Sainsbury's – from the administrator. This significant move will give us a real chance to develop our brand in supermarkets, while creating a substantial dry cleaning and photo business – further evidence that each year brings even more ways to grow our company.

We have strayed a long way from the shoe shop my grandfather opened in l869. But the principles are the same. He would be amazed to find he has started a business that is now repairing watches. He would be staggered to discover we even own a pub. The White Eagle at Rhoscolyn, although very successful, is definitely not the start of a chain. Yet even at the pub we have created success by trusting the staff that look after the customers, and I'm pretty sure great-grandpa would approve of that.

Chapter 3
HIGH STREET CASUALTIES

Recently I looked back at the high street of my youth. Among our archives are pictures of old Timpson shoe shops taken in the 1940s and 1950s. It wasn't just our shops that interested me; I was fascinated by the ones next door. Lots of once-famous names, such as Timothy White & Taylor and Hepworth's, have disappeared. I obtained some old street trading plans that showed the occupants of each shop in 1967 – the year I started as ladies' shoe buyer at Timpson. Roughly 75 per cent of the stores have gone out of business.

In the 1960s there were lots of multiple tailors: Willoughby, Alexandre, Hepworth, Harry Fenton, Jacksons the Tailor, Dunns, Horne Brothers, Hector Powe, Weaver to Wearer, and John Collier.

I witnessed the demise of John Collier at first hand. In 1973, after Timpson had been sold to the UDS Group, I was appointed the first (and last) shoe buyer at UDS Tailoring, which included Alexandre, Claude Alexander and John Collier. I was there for six months. Most John Collier units occupied prominent high street positions with an enormous ground floor given over to a big window display and a made-to-measure department. Shirts, shoes, socks and ready-to-wear clothes were sold upstairs. But it was made-to-measure that was big business. Spurred on by advertis ing, 90 per cent of the chain's turnover came from made-to-measure suits. (In those days, every one had a suit for best. Not only was it standard dress for weddings, funerals and church on Sundays but some people even wore their suit when they went to the beach on their annual holiday. Lots of faithful customers bought a new John Collier suit for Christmas.)

John Collier, previously called the "Fifty Shilling Tailor," offered three-piece suits at £17.99 made from a wide range of cloth designs. A customer's measurements were sent to a John Collier factory in Yorkshire or the north-east; the finished garment was returned to the shop ready for collection within a fortnight.

When I joined, business was booming. There was no hint of the revolution that was just around the corner. Yet within ten years the made-to-measure suit business had all but disappeared. Rapid changes in lifestyle and fashion led to demand for a more casual look and for ready-to-wear. By 1988, the John Collier name had completely disappeared from the high street.

The only big chain that did move with the times was Ralph Halpern's Burton Group. Burton did reinvent its business. Every shop was refitted. The made-to-measure bar was thrown out in favour of jackets, trousers and shirts sold by self-selection.

The approach was so successful that Burton acquired several competitors and extended its approach to womenswear. It took over well-known names such as Peter Robinson and Dorothy Perkins. It invented a new format, Topshop, which was a runaway success. Not only had Burton discovered self-service but it knew how to cater for an emerging fashion market. Rival fashion chains began to look middle-aged and eventually disappeared. In our archives I found a picture of a Timpson shop wedged between Hepworth and Kendall Rainwear. Both businesses eventually became part of another high street revolution.

In 1979 Hepworth was the third biggest menswear chain, behind Burton and John Collier. Under its chairman Terence Conran – whose Habitat shops were creating their own high street revolution – and development director Trevor Morgan, they recruited a young fashion entrepreneur called George Davies. Kendall Rainwear provided them with the opportunity to create a new business. It seems amazing today that a chain of shops selling

mackintoshes could be profitable, but Kendall Rainwear was not alone –
it had a competitor called Direct Raincoat. As more people drove cars and
stopped waiting at bus stops, coat sales fell and Kendall made losses. Its 95
branches were then bought by Hepworth. Within six months, all of them
had been turned into the very first Next shops. The new chain was so successful that within five years all Hepworth shops had been closed and converted into bigger Next stores.

In the 1960s and 1970s, the world of shoe shops remained largely un-
affected by the retail revolution. There always seemed to be too many of
them. On one street plan I found seven shoe shops next to each other. (I
recently invented a shoe shop game: you name one chain and I have to
name another, to see how long we can keep going like that without repe-
tition. Once we listed 54 before we gave up; later I discovered that at least
75 shoe chains of over ten shops have traded in the UK during the past 30
years. Here is a reminder to get you started: Olivers, Lennards, Easiphit,
Tylers, Lotus, Peter Lord, K Shoes, Milwards, Bata, Playfair, Hiltons, Norvic, and don't forget Timpson!)

When I started work in 1960, Timpson was an extremely strong business. It was a household name in the north of England and Scotland. Even
today many people remember being taken by their parents to buy their
shoes at the local Timpson shop.

The second generation of Timpson management – my grandfather
Will and his half-brother Noel – provided inspired leadership. They had
all it takes to make a success of a retail business. They totally understood
their market; they knew how to follow fashion; they had a particularly
good eye for property; and my grandfather, in particular, possessed the
personal touch that made him a hero in the eyes of his employees.

My father and his cousin, who took over the reins in 1960, were com-
petent but not inspirational. The business stopped growing and they failed
to develop the company's property portfolio. It was a time of rapid change
on the high street with a lot of rebuilding after the Second World War.
Timpson didn't have the courage to take the more expensive larger and
well-sited shops necessary to retain its position as a market leader. Nervous
of high rents, they tentatively acquired 20ft frontages instead of 40ft and
concentrated on acquisitions in the industrial north where unemployment

was increasing. They failed to make their mark in the prosperous south.

When I started to run the business in 1975, Timpson was still profitable but had slipped well down the pecking order. It was nothing like the force it had been at the end of the 1950s.

By the mid-1980s it was clear that shoe retailing was heading for trouble. For years there had been too many shoe shops; suddenly we found that even more shops were selling shoes. The Burton Group introduced shoe concessions and this technique was copied by other clothes retailers. The arrival of trainers took 25 per cent of the footwear market and most of that was being gobbled up by the emerging sports shops. The list of problems went on. Shoe retailing takes up a lot of space and, at a time when rental values were rising rapidly, our profits were being squeezed. We couldn't recover the extra rent by increasing prices because the rising tide of imports was forcing prices down. Wage rates were rising. Ten per cent of shoes were being bought through mail order. The British Shoe Corporation (BSC) had acquired over 25 per cent of the market. For a business such as Timpson, it was almost impossible to increase sales.

Having led a management buyout of Timpson, the business was heavily geared. It was also paying full rents as it did not have a freehold portfolio of properties. These conditions made me face reality, probably more quickly than many. I saw the impending demise of the traditional high street shoe shop and sold the business to Olivers in 1987. Olivers, itself, has now disappeared, having been acquired in 2001. (The shops now trade under the name Shoe Zone.)

By 1985 I thought it inevitable that a lot of the high street shoe chains would disappear. But I didn't envisage the rapid demise of the dominant British Shoe Corporation (BSC). BSC had been built up in the 1950s and 1960s by Charles Clore and Harry Levison. Clore was a genius at property, spotting the freehold value of multiple businesses, buying them on the cheap and using the property assets to fund his future investment. He built up the Sears Holdings retail empire: this controlled more than 26 per cent of the UK footwear market but also Lewis's department stores (which then included Selfridges), the fashion chain Wallis, Foster Brothers Menswear, Olympus Sports, Milletts, Adams Childrenswear, Horne Brothers, Mappin & Webb and William Hill.

Clore left the development of his shoe business to Harry Levison, whose own company Clerkenwell Footwear was developed into the national chain Curtess. Through a series of acquisitions, several well-known high street names became part of BSC – Freeman Hardy & Willis, True Form, Manfield, Saxone, Dolcis, Lilley & Skinner, Roland Cartier, Cable, Benefit and Phillips' Character Shoes. Levison developed probably the best buying team that had ever served a retail business. They were so dominant on the high street that some consumers accused them of controlling fashion. This was not true; their buyers were so good that they predicted fashion better than anyone else has done before or since.

When Levison retired in the late 1970s he handed over the management of BSC to Harry Harrison, an operations man trained at Littlewoods. Although he had little buying expertise, Harrison knew the business well enough to allow the buying team to flourish. Sadly, he died within two years of taking over.

The business was then run by David Roberts, who was a talented menswear buyer but without the qualities to make a good managing director. But he still had a really large business: it was bigger than Marks & Spencer and Woolworths combined, although it had reached its peak.

David Roberts's successor, Chris Marsland, was an operations man. He brought a more systematic approach to the buying department. Flair was replaced by computers, and the buyers, controlled by merchandisers, were told how many to buy.

It was an unhappy development. Some of the buyers left and others were asked to leave. Within two years BSC had lost its major strength; the best buying team in the country had been replaced by a computer.

The new team believed their market dominance had been obtained by having the biggest centralised warehouse system in Europe. They had forgotten that the most important thing in a shoe shop is to have shoes that people want to buy.

As things started to go wrong in BSC, trouble also emerged at the holding company Sears. After Charles Clore's death, all appeared to go well for a time under the control of Geoffrey Maitland-Smith and Michael Pickard. They eventually decided to appoint Liam Strong, the marketing director of British Airways, as the new chief executive.

I went to see Liam Strong in 1987, shortly after I had sold our shoe shops. As I was no longer a competitor, I was able to offer advice on the footwear retail scene. He was in a buoyant mood. He suggested that I meet Ian Thompson, his new managing director of BSC. So I had tea with Ian and he told me about his plans. "All I am going to do is go for the easy wins," he said.

BSC had just carried out an experiment, converting one of its shops in St Helens to a new fascia called Shoe Express. It was a concept copied from Payless, a successful US shoe chain, and was an immediate success. This wasn't surprising because it had been spoon-fed with all the best stock that BSC could offer, providing customers with every size and every colour in all the bestsellers. That was Ian's first easy win. He was going to convert shops to the Shoe Express format as fast as he could.

The other easy win in his eyes was Dolcis, which still retained a dominant position in the young fashion market for footwear.

For a time they produced success but it was only just enough to compensate for the deterioration of the rest of the business. After two years it became clear that Shoe Express was not such an easy win after all.

By the time Ian Thompson had been succeeded by two other managing directors, BSC was in freefall. It panicked. Freeman Hardy & Willis, True Form and Saxone were sold in a strange hire-purchase type deal to Stephen Hinchcliffe, an entrepreneur who had started to build up a portfolio of loss-making shops despite having insufficient financial backing and little retail experience. His chains included Sock Shop and Salisbury's Handbags but the BSC shops accounted for the greatest part of his turnover. Hinchcliffe then went bust in a big way and BSC had to take back a large part of the portfolio.

In the end things got so bad that Sears called in the company doctor David James (who subsequently conducted the autopsy on the Millennium Dome). He sold the rump of BSC to Philip Green, who used it to build a cash mountain for the future purchase of BhS and Arcadia. In five years BSC had gone from 26 per cent of the footwear retail market to nothing.

My study of the high street of the 1960s revealed other lost, once-prominent names. Collingwoods the jewellers became a part of Next. Ratners disappeared for other reasons (after its brand was besmirched by

Gerald Ratner's infamous speech to the Institute of Directors), although many of the shops still remain trading under the H Samuel fascia.

Perhaps the biggest change was in food retailing. Every high street had its MacFisheries and Dewhurst the butcher. There were several general multiple food retailers such as Liptons, Maypole, International Stores, Home & Colonial and Seymour Mead. Today almost all this trade is done in out-of-town supermarkets, but most of those names had disappeared long before, acquired by emerging chains such as Tesco and Gateway (now Somerfield).

Television was a novelty when my historic pictures were taken. Radio Rentals, Telefusion, Granada and Martin Dawes (the only name that still survives) catered for people who paid for their television by weekly rental. Technology and lifestyle have left these businesses behind.

In the 1950s almost every high street had a Singer shop selling sewing machines and a range of cottons. Today, it seems amazing that anyone could make a retail business out of such a narrow product range. Maybe in 20 years' time we will find it just as strange that there were shops that simply sold mobile phones.

Today, you wouldn't expect to find furniture, carpets and DIY shops on the high street. In 1955 you could buy three-piece suites from Cantors, New Day and Times Furnishing; carpets from Cyril Lord; and wallpaper from Crown Wallpaper shops. Timothy White's, otherwise known as Timothy White & Taylor, was acquired in the 1960s by Boots, which used the larger shops to make a dramatic improvement to its property portfolio. We ate at Charles Forte's ice cream shops, Lyons' Corner House and Wimpy Bars.

High street names continue to appear and disappear. Ethel Austin, Music Zone and Dolcis are some recent examples. It's a safe bet that, during the next 45 years, at least 80 per cent of the names here today will also go. It makes you wonder what we have got to do to survive.

It's surprising that a multiple shoe repairer exists at all. Since 1965, 90 per cent of the shoe repair trade has gone. When I started, most towns would have ten or even 15 shoe repairers; the best of those would employ 20 operatives. In the 1960s there were plenty of repair chains: Shoe Craft, Paynes, Coombes, Modern Shoe Repairs, Malones, Broughalls, Norman Sweet, Automagic, Mr Minit and, of course, Timpson. We are the only name left. The purpose of this book is to help us keep our name there.

The business was started by William Timpson in the 1860s. His first shop in Oldham Street, Manchester, was an immediate success. He used his profits to grow the business, opening more shops around Manchester before expanding to Liverpool, Sheffield, Northamptonshire and beyond. He started a shoe repair service in 1905; this was expanded to all shops over the following 15 years.

Above: Together, Hepworths and Kendall Rainwear created one of the biggest high street successes. In 1979 Hepworths' non-executive director Trevor Morgan bought Kendall's 110 shops, and George Davis joined the Hepworth team. Six months later, all the Kendall shops were converted into the first Next outlets. The concept was so successful that, two years later, the whole Hepworth chain was converted to the Next format. (Trevor Morgan was chairman of Timpson between 1983 and 1985.)

Opposite: Menswear retailers, which had prospered in the previous decades, found the 1970s traumatic. Before then, most men bought made-to-measure suits; an order placed on Saturday would be ready for collection ten days later.

In 1995, the British Shoe Corporation had a 25 per cent share of the UK shoe retail market, owning Freeman, Hardy & Willis, Trueform, Saxone, Dolcis, Lilley & Skinner, Curtess, Manfield, Cable and Shoe Express. Within five years, all those shops had either been sold or closed down – and the British Shoe Corporation had disappeared.

41

Until 1967, the shoe repair work in a Timpson shop was separated from the shop reception. Customers were served by counter girls; the cobblers never saw a customer.

1980

1987

Over the past 20 years, the Timpson business has grown from 150 outlets to more than 630 via a series of acquisitions.

shoe repairs // the menders
1989

Automagic the shoe repairers
while you wait service
1995

Shoe Service • Keys • Travel Goods

Dry cleaning
2008

MISTER MINIT Shoe Service • Keys • Travel Goods
Shoe Repair
2003

TIMOTHY WHITES

CHEMISTS

LIPTON

J. LYONS & Cº.

Scotch Wool Shop

RADIO RENTALS

CASHIER

FINLAY & Cº. LTD.
TOBACCONISTS

SINGER

DEWHURST

PAIGE

SALISBURYS

SWEARS & WELLS Hundreds of high street names have failed to pass the test of time, no matter how well-known. It's a reminder that nothing is forever. Today, you can't find many TV rental shops, tobacconists or multiple butchers, or shops such as Swears & Wells that specialised in selling fur coats.

Chapter 4

WHY ARE WE THE SURVIVORS?

When I started, the shoe repair market was ten times bigger than it is today. Shoes were repaired in big factories employing 20 or more people. Customers never saw a shoe repairer. In the 1950s a lot of our business came from local shoe shops and major industrial customers. We had big contracts with the police and the fire brigade.

The traditional back street cobbler started to suffer when the winkle picker and stiletto fashion produced heel bars and more shoe repairers opened on the high street. Within ten years most of the big shoe repair factories had been wiped out, both by these new competitors and by major changes in shoe construction.

Businesses founded on repairing British-made leather shoes had no place in a world full of imported footwear made of synthetic materials that were considerably cheaper and much harder wearing.

Those factories that survived the 1960s faced another problem. During a period of high inflation, low-paid workers received wage increases of up to 50 per cent – a substantial increase to the wage bill that put a lot of cobblers out of business.

Since 1975 most shoe repairing has been done on the high street. Thirty years ago, there were lots of successful multiple shoe repair companies. None have survived except for Timpson. Some didn't react to the changing market. Others suffered when control was transferred to the next generation of family ownership. We gained insights into the reasons behind the demise of the shoe repair multiples from the history of those businesses that we have acquired since 1980.

FAMILY FAILURE

Based in Luton, W H Broughall was a second-generation family business run by three brothers and a sister. They had 35 shops, mainly in good sites spreading from Cheltenham to Norwich. But in 1980 the business was in trouble. I met some of the family members in a pub near Dunstable to discuss a possible purchase. It was a long, liquid lunch – something that some of the brothers clearly regarded as routine. Day-to-day control was left to their sister while the brothers enjoyed living off the business.

Shortly after we had bought the business, their area manager, Ralph Young, told me about one particular Thursday when the brothers had gone to Monte Carlo for a weekend at the casinos. By Friday afternoon they were running out of money. They had phoned Ralph and told him to go round as many shops as possible. His instructions: "Take the money out of the till and catch a plane to Monte Carlo." Ralph delivered the money. Within two hours, he was back on the next plane home to England.

On my first visit to the Broughall shop in Witney, I arrived to find the door locked and a notice saying "back at 3.30pm". After a 15-minute wait the manager arrived, carrying his weekly shopping. It is a big branch in a prime spot but his total sales for the previous week were only £270. We still trade in the same site; it has an average weekly turnover of £6,700.

OVER-STRETCHED MANAGEMENT

In 1980 we bought 12 shops in Kent called Shoe Care. They were trading well but Brian Smith, the owner, had no children to succeed him. He decided that the business had reached its limit. He didn't want to expand out of Kent or appoint a second area manager (the opening of a second shop and the appointment of a second area manager are two of the most critical steps in the growth of a new retail business).

Another successful management team that decided to cash in were

John Stratford and Chris Fowler, who had developed Shoetech. The partners were based in Jersey where they already had a good shoe repair business before exporting their concept to the mainland. They had created a modern shoe repair/key cutting business and knew how to choose good sites. Every branch was doing extremely well but they found it difficult to manage 12 shops stretching from Cardiff to Crawley. We paid them a good price for the business; they continue to run their shops in the Channel Islands.

Lilleywhites, based in Yorkshire, was another company that found it difficult to manage shops that were far from home. On the strength of some good shoe repair units in Leeds and York, they took on a number of concessions in Johnsons the Cleaners. The concessions were as far away as Bangor in North Wales. All had small turnovers and each only needed one operative. Providing staff cover was a nightmare, and standards of quality and service suffered. When we bought the shops, they were quick to benefit from our mobile management team.

LOST INSIDE A CORPORATE EMPIRE

Many multiple footwear retailers that grew rapidly during the 1950s introduced a shoe repair service. Several, such as Clarks, had their own factories. But once shoe repairing started to decline, most, quite rightly, decided to stick to their core business and leave shoe repairing to specialists. The giant of the footwear trade, British Shoe Corporation (BSC), however, retained some shoe repair factories. Most were inside shoe shops, although some had separate entrances. BSC also had shoe repair concessions within department stores such as Lewis's, Selfridges, the Co-op and some independents.

It was almost impossible to develop a good key-cutting and merchandise business for a shoe repairer hidden in a shoe shop. The Menders, the BSC shoe repair business, became forgotten inside a big business that was, itself, in trouble. It must have been a lonely job for the operatives running branches that took in no more than £600 per week. The business relied heavily on its star performer in Selfridges (which was the main reason we bought the business).

The operatives needed love but they didn't get it. The business was run on dictatorial lines. Although there were only 50 shops, the general manager Arthur Hudson visited less than half of them every year.

DICTATORIAL MANAGEMENT

While many chains floundered, Automagic flourished. This company was born in the stiletto boom and was the first chain to make a real success in London. Managing director Mike Strom developed the business with his partner Paul Lister. Strom was the shoe repairer; Lister the property man and strategist.

Early in the 1980s, Lister wanted to cash in. It was decided to float the company. At the same time, Automagic moved from its London head office in Kings Cross to a £1m building in Harpenden that eventually became a financial burden.

While business was still healthy they bought Norman Sweet, a 12-shop multiple in the West Country. It was an excellent purchase, adding a number of profitable sites to their portfolio, including several with extremely good engraving and trophy businesses.

Mike Strom's heart was in London and his real love was shoe repairs. The London shops also enjoyed substantial turnover from dry cleaning – with the work being contracted out to a third party. Eventually, Strom tried to increase margins by acquiring the London dry cleaner Swiss Hand Services. But this proved to be a particularly costly move; mounting Swiss Hand Service losses made a substantial dent in Automagic's core business performance.

Fran Donaghy, who is currently one of our area development managers for Edinburgh and north-east England, left Timpson in 1984 because of the opportunities with Automagic. We were paying him £80 per week plus £6 bonus; Automagic offered him £100 base plus a £100 guaranteed bonus. He opened the branch in Middlesbrough. It was a great success, earning him even more each week than the £200 he expected. "For the next few years it was a great formula," Fran recalls, "but when stilettos went out of fashion Automagic never re-invested. The shop didn't change from the day it opened. Its brown hessian walls and cream paint looked drab as the years passed by. Gradually the feeling of success was replaced by nit-picking management. Our telephone was adjusted to prevent outgoing calls, so we were constantly visiting the phone box. Petty cash was limited to £5. Stock failed to arrive. We couldn't get hold of anyone to help with our problems but when we had a poor week we received threatening letters."

Ralph O'Brien, who I recently met in our new branch in Hillsborough, was managing an Automagic unit in Meadowhall Shopping Centre when we purchased the company in 1995. "I got one pay rise in five years," remembers Ralph. "They just didn't listen. A lot of the problems were caused by Swiss Hand Services. This put the business in debt to the tune of £1m and Mike Strom didn't know how to get out of it."

Tony Sharpe, one of our three regional managers, joined Automagic in 1986. In the mid-1980s he was earning £15,000 a year which, at the age of 21, was pretty good going.

The job was fun," he recalls. "I was keen to develop the business so I copied the sandwich board outside the Timpson shop, which put pet tags on one side and keys on the other. Our key cutting sales went up by 50 per cent. Then I met Mike Strom. He was probably his own worst enemy. He didn't like my sandwich board. He said the increase in sales was a coincidence. I was to take the board upstairs and never put it out again. But I did – and sales continued to flourish.

"Mike Strom rang me a couple of weeks later. He asked me whether the keyboard was still out. I lied and said no. 'I told you sales wouldn't go back down if you took it away,' he said. He didn't like copying Timpson. The key cutting promotion was a real obsession for him."

In 1993 Tony applied to be an area manager. "I hadn't got a clue how the business was doing because they only sent one newsletter a year," he says. "I soon discovered other shops were not the same as mine. Frankly, the people were not very good. The overall business wasn't much good, either. Other area managers were jumping ship, so my area increased in size almost monthly. I was going as far as Peterborough and Norwich but most of my time was spent telling people they were redundant.

"No one was allowed to spend any money. No new Hoovers. No window cleaners. One of my jobs was to fit a lock to every phone. We had to work every Saturday, and at 8.30am I went to a phone box to check every shop was open (I carried a bag of ten pence pieces for the purpose). If a blade broke on the key machine, branches could only order a replacement on the following Friday. So the branches ordered more blades than necessary. The weekly bonus was capped at £180. A new super monthly bonus was added but hardly anyone ever reached their target.

"Mike Strom visited shops but he would not listen when he got there. Paul Lister was the clever guy and when he left the decline started. In his annual report, Strom always had an excuse for last year's poor performance – the weather, bombs in London, strikes or stilettos.

"Eventually I realised that he wanted to put his successful London formula into the rest of the country. Because London did well with umbrellas, umbrellas were stocked everywhere. Mike Strom loved shoe care products. He insisted every branch had a wall-to-wall display of shoe polish, laces and insoles. Some branches took £700 a week. It was a good business but it got in the way of key cutting (in London, key cutting was a very small part of the business). We stopped opening new shops. We never had any refits except when shops were cut down in size to reduce our rent.

"Dishonesty continued by default. Automagic was reluctant to fire anyone for stealing. Its policy was 'we're lucky to have the staff so we can't afford to get rid of them'. The stock control system caused lots of problems. Instead of placing an order, you sent head office a list of your stock holding and the computer decided what you needed. But the computer didn't understand the seasons. So we got shoe whitener in the autumn and weather protector in the summer. You had to beat the computer by lying about your stock.

"Looking back at it," says Tony, "there was no strategy. It was a dictatorial management with head office blaming everyone but themselves. I just wanted an end to it. I was in Tenerife on holiday when the end came. When I got back I found I was working for Dennis Birkin, Timpson's Area Manager."

MR MINIT

In the 1960s and 70s the biggest shoe repair chain was Allied Shoe Repairs (ASR), a subsidiary of the leather supplier Allied Leather, which had acquired a number of shoe repair chains, including Malones, Shoecraft and Paynes. The biggest part of ASR was Coombes, which had been founded in 1889 by James Coombes in Hull. His aim was simple: he wanted to become Britain's largest shoe repairer and he had definite ideas on the best way to go about achieving this aim. He realised the importance of gimmicks, attracting customers by giving away free packets of tea. Above all, he set out to sell a service.

By the end of the 19th century, Coombes was one of the largest independent chains in the country. When the company celebrated its 75th anniversary in 1964, it had more than 300 branches and was Britain's largest shoe repairer. It was halfway into a programme of enabling all branches to provide a full repair on a while-you-wait basis. Shops sold polishes, laces and other shoe sundries but also leather travel goods, handbags and wallets. By the early 1970s, Coombes had joined ASR and grown to 500 branches.

Within ASR, chairman Fergus Watson and managing director Lawrence Hardy kept the original name of each chain on the fascia and gave local management considerable freedom. Although ASR added key cutting and engraving to its shops, it was leather goods that provided the cushion when shoe repair sales fell.

Coombes's valuable property portfolio gave strength to Allied's balance sheet, helping to hold its share value on the stock market. But with profits stagnant and the prospect of a further shoe repair decline, Allied Leather decided to concentrate on its core leather business. ASR was bought by Mr Minit in 1985.

Mr Minit had been started in 1957 by Donald Hilsden-Ryan with a heel bar in a Brussels department store. His timing was perfect. Stilettos were coming into fashion and his little booths were highly successful. Over the next 30 years, the Minit brand was introduced throughout Europe as well as into Australia, New Zealand, Japan and Canada. By the time Minit acquired ASR in 1985, it owned about 4,000 shops.

Previously, Minit had expanded into the UK by buying Hennessey, a business that operated heel bars in Woolworths with a heavy emphasis on key cutting and engraving. ASR must have been a big shock for Minit. Instead of acquiring more heel bars, it had bought shops carrying lots of merchandise.

Sensibly, Minit didn't try to convert the ASR stores to the Minit formula. David Short, their managing director in the late 1980s, introduced three retail formats: Saddlers, an up-market cobbler; Mr Minit heel bars; and Gulliver's for luggage, with shoe repair and key cutting services at the back. Although profits didn't progress, the business plan kept central management in Brussels happy.

David Short was replaced by Kenn Begley, who introduced Hilsden-Ryan to Ian Siddall of the investment bank UBS. In 1997 UBS bought the entire Minit business for an estimated £75m. Although the UK part of Minit only produced £1m of its worldwide £13m profits, Siddall decided to use the UK as the base for a new global brand. Within 18 months he had bought InTime, a watch repair chain, and the troubled Sketchley and SupaSnaps businesses. (That deal cost a modest £2m but also included a £50m guarantee to pay future rent liabilities.)

With consultants and professional managers, Siddall developed Minit Solutions, a one-stop high street service shop. The strategy seemed good but missed a vital point. Customers not only want good design and every service under one roof; they also want to be served by staff with the expertise to do a good job.

I remember visiting a Minit Solutions in a Sainsbury's store outside Newbury. I asked the girl behind the counter whether she could cut my key.

"No," she said.

"Why?" I asked.

"We haven't had the training yet," she said. "But I am on a course on Friday, so I could cut your key next week."

In four years Minit UK lost £120m. The concept didn't work and management blamed the staff. "We have a great formula," the management said. "If everyone pursues their individual objectives, the project will be a great success."

Senior management fell in love with Minit Solutions. They couldn't afford for the concept to fail. There was a succession of managing directors but none were shoe repairers. Most of them brought in other people, who also knew nothing about the industry, to help them fix the problem.

Area managers came from unrelated businesses such as Burtons, Somerfield, Thomas Cook and Dorothy Perkins. None of them could get their mind around managing shoe repairers. They couldn't believe a shoe repairer should run a shop so Minit Solution units were managed by graduates.

Minit had lost touch with reality. Each week, its branches would ring the area manager who had left a message about trading performance on his answerphone. James somehow obtained the area managers' phone numbers, so we at Timpson could listen to Minit's latest news.

Another answerphone saga is a sad comment on their management style. A round of SupaSnap closures was about to be announced; each branch was given a special number to ring on a Friday afternoon. Those ringing one number were told about the closure plan while those given the other number were told they were being made redundant.

After a number of strategic reviews and the closure of 400 shops, Minit finally realised they had got it wrong. They sold us the business for £1, handing over tax losses of £120m.

The first three months after we bought Minit were difficult. Minit people didn't trust us – management had been given a bad name.

"There were lots of negative vibes," recalls area manager Andy Willingham, who was given the job of meeting some Minit people on the day we took over. "It was difficult to convince them we were any better than the lot they had before. It took four months before anyone from Minit realised how good it could be."

"The way they ran it was black and white," confirmed Martin Wainwright, when I met him at our Long Eaton branch. "They were management and they gave the orders. The area managers knew about shops but not our type of shop."

"Just before you took over," said Gary Thompson, "my shop was about to become a Minit Solutions, and I was being demoted to number three. They were bringing in a proper manager who couldn't repair a shoe." (Gary is now doing an extremely good job developing our turnover at Carlisle.)

I realised the strength of feeling among Minit employees during one of my discussion groups. Most of the meeting was taken up with stories of Minit's management.

"The whole business was about cost-cutting," said one. "And the most ridiculous scheme was the ban on buying postage stamps. To get a stamp we had to go through our anchor branch who contacted the area manager who spoke to the district auditor who sent us the stamps in the post."

Paul Masters, our manager in Coventry, summarised the difference between Minit and Timpson.

"I like the way you allow us to get on with it," he says. "Minit shot themselves in the foot with their tills. These fixed our prices. Instructions were sent to the tills every Saturday night. One week they increased prices by 20 per cent without telling us they were carrying out a trial. Keys suddenly went from £4 to £4.80 but we didn't find out until we put the first sale through the till. The trial lasted four weeks until they discovered sales had dropped dramatically. When you threw out our EPOS tills, it gave us the right message: we were back in charge. Minit people started to realise you would make a difference."

Davie Thomson, who runs our shop in Lanark, remembers: "I dropped my basic pay when Timpson took over but the bonus made it much better. The Minit bonus was useless. I was set an impossible target. It did my head in. The issue of those postage stamps will always stick in my mind. After UBS took over Minit, it really went wrong, especially after it bought SupaSnaps. The SupaSnaps woman became our area manager; she didn't know anything about our business but lasted over a year. Our previous area manager knew the business inside out but he was paid off."

CONCLUSIONS

Plenty of competitors have disappeared during the past 30 years. They have taught us many lessons. So why have we survived?

It is easy to point to the deals: leading the management buyout, selling the shoe shops, buying Automagic and Minit and then selling Sketchley. They all made a big difference to our profits.

We have certainly had a lot of luck.

It is easy to be critical in hindsight when a business has failed, but we had many advantages over our opposition.

Selling the Timpson shoe shops set Timpson Shoe Repairs free to go its own way. The shoe repair operation in BSC did not have that chance.

When we decided to throw out merchandise and go for key cutting, Minit could have done the same – but it was held back by its reliance on leather goods.

Maybe we were lucky to forecast the decline in shoe repairs, as that made us so determined to increase the number of our services. If Automagic had done the same, it would probably have been more successful than Timpson.

But the biggest difference between us isn't luck. It's simply that we have had better people, and have looked after them. We visited our branches and listened to what they had to say.

Thanks to our acquisitions, we now have a great property portfolio. And we have a management team to match it, led by James who is as enthusiastic as I ever was and even more ambitious.

It helps to be neurotic. If you are worried about the business when it is going well, you will find ways to make it even better and make it grow. The joy of growing the business gives me more pleasure than any material things, so I'd rather invest profits back in the business.

INVESTMENT

For 20 years, we have been determined to diversify to protect the business against our forecast fall in the demand for shoe repairs. Our biggest investments have been Automagic and Mr Minit, but the most important capital spend is on refits. We must keep our shops up-to-date and remember that branch colleagues rely on the continual year-on-year success of their branch to increase their bonus. Our branches have been refitted every seven years. We keep replacing our key cutting machinery, invest in computer engravers and we back every service with its own specialist workshop.

The biggest investment of all is in training. We make money by providing a skilled service. Without the skills, we haven't got a business. Top of the training list is customer care. Good quality craftsmen make a difference, but the colleagues who take the most money are excellent at looking after customers. Every retailer claims good customer service as a high priority, but a lot aren't good at putting it into practice. I don't just look for good customer care. I want customers to think we are great.

MANAGEMENT STYLE

Our management style has made a big difference. Each year people tell me how much they like upside-down management. "It's more relaxed," some say. "I can be my own boss," say others, "but there is always someone there to help me and it gives me a chance to prove what I can do."

We first introduced upside-down management in Scotland when we realised that Scottish shops want to be run by Scots. Scotland is different. Its schools start on a different date. It has its own bank holidays. Scots buy loads of nameplates, as many Scots live in tenement blocks and put their surname on the door to help the postman. We have always had a Scottish area manager to run Scotland and we also now have a Scottish regional manager. I do not, however, expect this policy to extend to the role of the chairman...

Upside-down management relies on good people. One of the best decisions we made was to stop employing shoe repairers. For ten years we have recruited personalities and then taught them the skills. Our increased turnover and profit reflects the better calibre of our people.

SECURITY

Our approach to theft has made a difference. Twenty years ago we thought it okay; if the thief wasn't too greedy, we let him get away with it. The experience of Automagic in London changed our minds. There, it wasn't just petty theft; it was organised crime. Kenn Begley of Minit introduced me to hidden cameras and since then our security officer, Paul Myatt, has turned catching thieves into an art form.

PEOPLE

But it isn't luck or major decisions that make the biggest difference. It's people. Here are just some stories of our star performers. They give an idea of the contributions that people can make.

Mike Frank was the general manager of Timpson Shoe Repairs for 20 years until he retired in 1987. He had a traditional management style and was most comfortable when everyone followed a rigid set of rules. He meticulously inspected shops to ensure everyone toed the line. That style is very different from Timpson today but it worked because Mike was passionate about the business. Thanks to him, the company survived a turbulent time when two takeover bids and a major decline in shoe repairs could have led to disaster. When Mike retired he handed over the perfect platform for future growth.

Kit Green first worked for Timpson as a marketing graduate in the early 1970s. He left when we were bought by UDS but we kept in touch. He returned when the shoe repair business was going through a difficult time in 1985, taking over as its managing director after we sold the shoe shops. To some, Kit was too laid back – but he was a listener and a thinker. He taught the business how to get its priorities right. "Do the simple things," he said, "just do what matters most."

Alan Chatterton was an unconventional, untrained enthusiast who rose from the administration office to the boardroom because he so passionately believed in the business. Alan taught me the art of the possible. On one occasion I rang him at 9pm on a Sunday.

"We need to go to Kent tomorrow," I said.

"No problem," was his immediate reply. "Where and when do you want to meet?"

At 6am the following morning, he was at Crewe Station.

Alan was the *Mastermind* of the shoe repair industry. He didn't just know all our shops, he knew every competitor as well, because he travelled the country two or three days every week. He taught us a lot about the way to run a business.

Perry Watkins is still embarrassed when he sees photographs of himself as a scruffy lad running our shop in Aylesbury but he has come a long way since those days. In his present role he is in charge of our field operations. He got there because he was our most successful area manager and regional manager. His success is based on respect; Perry looks after his people and fights for them and makes sure the business makes their lives better. That's why they trust him.

Sid Hubbard is the youngest area manager that we have ever appointed. He has shown more maturity than most I can remember. Sid has already done a lot to improve our business. We have given him tough areas to run because we know he is up for a challenge. He has shown us how professional our area role has become and further strengthened my view that all area managers should be internal appointments.

Gail Cobb is a member of a large group who have worked for us for more than 25 years. She is also part of an elite gang of girls who work in our finance department. Gail runs payroll and has been doing so for 15 years. She always seems unflappable. Even when the acquisition of Minit threw her life into turmoil, she looked as calm as ever. For years I have been trying to eliminate the term "head office" and instead talk about "Timpson House" as the place that provides a service to branches. Gail was doing that well before I even thought of the idea.

John Tucker ran our shop in Merthyr Tydfil, a little Portakabin outside Asda at the top of a hill. Then he became area development manager – a role sadly brought to an end by his premature death. Before John died, he played a critical part in the development of our training. I wanted manuals that had pictures and very few words. I decided John was the man who could create them. We met at a hotel just off junction 8 of the M6. He hadn't a clue what I was going to ask but he took it in his stride. Within three months he had written his first easy-to-read training manual.

Peter Harris joined Timpson as a management trainee and, after surviving a spell assisting some of our toughest area managers, took on the responsibility for training. For the past ten years, Peter has used the full force of his strong personality to promote Timpson training. In difficult times many companies cut the training budget. I wouldn't like to be around if you try that on Peter.

John Quantrill joined us from the Royal Navy as our establishment officer, looking after often tedious administration in the office and warehouse that served both our shoe shops and shoe repair business. It wasn't part of our original plan for John to transfer with the shoe repair business when we sold the shoe shops. Sensibly, we changed our minds and asked John to run the warehouse. For the next 19 years until his retirement, John consistently demonstrated that you can be nice and efficient at the same time. He showed us all that being unselfish is a great way to gain respect.

These are just a few of our star performers. There are lots more. The most significant number of them work in our branches. They are shop managers who have, through their skill and personality, created a big band of loyal Timpson customers. While our competitors fell by the wayside, these people made sure our business grew. That's why we have survived.

Chapter 5
WHAT OUR PEOPLE SAY (Part 1)

James had made it clear to me. The only way to understand why our culture works was to talk to our people. So I followed his advice.

I arranged meetings to fit in with my shop visit routine. (I spend about seven days every month visiting branches, seeing every shop over an 18-month cycle.) For two months I carried an A4 pad, specifically searching for the reasons behind our success. I kept asking the same questions: "What do you think about Timpson? Why are we successful?"

I started enquiries in the Metro Centre, Gateshead. Why start there? Because I thought the north-eastern culture would be tough and even critical. The busiest shopping centre in the north-east is up the A1 beyond the fabulous Angel of the North. The free parking for customers is in stark contrast with the high rents we pay for our two units. I went to our larger shop, which is managed by Barbara Mead. I particularly wanted to meet her. Barbara has been with us for a generation and so was well-placed to comment on the fundamental changes that have made a difference to Timpson.

It was impossible to talk to Barbara in her busy shop – customers come first – so she and I went to the nearby McDonald's and made our coffees last nearly an hour. Her enthusiasm came as a bit of a surprise. She was much more positive than I had expected. She was also very thoughtful.

"I started in Grainger Street, Newcastle," she said. "For the first year I wasn't allowed to touch a shoe. I just did errands and cleaning. I joined when I was 16 and was nearly 21 before I served a customer. That was when the factory was moved into the shop downstairs and we started to provide a while-you-wait service. The old guys who had been there for years didn't like it. In those days, operatives specialised in different tasks – leather soles, rubber soles, heeling and finishing. The new set-up was in full view of the public, so shoe repairers had to be multi-skilled and sometimes even talk to a customer.

"Eventually I was moved to Sunderland where Alan White, the manager, taught me more about shoe repairs. I wasn't given a promotion, though, because women were not considered suitable to be relief managers. That old-fashioned view changed and so, at the age of 26 with ten years' experience, I was given my first management position in Eldon Square, Newcastle. I was a bit of a novelty. In those days very few women ran shops and," Barbara added, looking a little embarrassed, "I think I became a bit of a star. After a couple of years I was promoted to area development manager, helping to create computer engraving and watch repairs in the north-east. It was fun moving from shop to shop, helping develop something new. I continued this roving role until I became pregnant. After maternity leave, I settled here in the Metro Centre.

"I have seen a lot of changes during 24 years. In the old days, the branch manager was king. All information was hidden in a drawer. For years I never saw any figures, bonus calculations, or even the newsletter. We just did as we were told, kept our heads down and stopped for an hour for lunch at 12.30. The job has changed dramatically. The introduction of while-you-wait shoe repair machinery changed the whole way shoe repairers did the job. There was a massive improvement to our key cutting when the big keyboards were introduced. Computers completely changed engraving. But the biggest difference is the way you run the business. Now I am free to do what I want. I can use my ideas to run the branch and, if I have any problems, I just ring Andy, my area manager.

"I am pretty independent but I like Andy to check that my staff are as happy with me as I am with him. In the old days area managers – and I have worked for five of them – only talked to the manager. The rest of us might not have been there. Andy talks to everyone on each visit. If he didn't deal with my problems, I wouldn't hesitate to ring James. Some friends in other companies think it's odd that we can talk directly to senior management but it seems quite natural at Timpson. Today, when I told my team you were coming, George, who has just joined us, said, 'Wow, aren't you nervous?' 'Why should I be?' I explained. 'I have met John Timpson at least once a year for the past 20 years.'

"I trust Andy's judgment because he really knows the business. He used to run a shop himself and knows it isn't a doddle. Today, you have to be multi-skilled; you won't earn a big bonus just by being a benchman. We already have key cutting, engraving and watch repairs, and now you are introducing dry cleaning, jewellery repairs and photo ID. By developing the business, you are increasing our bonus. I believe in the art of the possible and like having a go at new things – that's how we learn."

Barbara looked seriously at me. "It's an interesting balance," she said, "because despite the freedom we get from upside-down management, we still need standards. We need to employ people who take pride in their job.

"Most of the people I worked with 24 years ago would never have survived the change. They were stuck in a rut. Today, the business is full of new ideas. We don't have an hour for dinner at 12.30 – we grab a break when it is quiet. We develop our business by looking after customers, not by sticking to rules laid down by head office. I like the way the business takes note of people in the shops. You have made it easier for us to make money. The bonus scheme creates the energy that makes our shops so buzzy. I started on £27.50 a week and now I get over £500. That shows how much the business has changed for the better."

SCOTLAND

The following week I visited Scotland. We have 75 shops in the country and many more Scottish colleagues run shops in England. Generally they provide high levels of discipline, housekeeping and salesmanship – but when I got to Inverness I was in for a shock.

I had flown up on the Sunday night in order to make an early morning visit. At 8.40am I was in Baron Taylor Street. It was 20 minutes before the shop was due to open and it looked a mess. A display board had been left outside over the weekend. The window featured holly and tinsel – but this was February. At 9.07am nobody had arrived. I rang Alex Barrett, the regional manager. "I am outside Baron Taylor Street," I said, "and it's shut." I walked off to visit our other Inverness shop in the precinct. When I returned at 9.30, the manager was there, claiming he had arrived at 9.05. I looked at the books. Sales were down by 50 per cent. I like disappointments; they show me how much better our business can become.

To be fair, it was an isolated incident. By the end of the day, after visiting Elgin, Peterhead and four shops in Aberdeen, I was in a much better mood. The highlight was my conversation with James Durno in the Trinity Centre, Aberdeen. James is a pretty hard-to-please guy. "Before I came here, I never stuck to a job for more than 18 months," he told me. "I've been here for four years and, I'm telling you, that says quite a lot. This upside-down management thing of yours certainly works for me. I'm free to do what I want and that's what I like."

Visiting shops around Edinburgh on the following day was even better. I was driven round by our ADM Fran Donaghy, who is lucky enough to live in the beautiful countryside near Galashiels. He was worried. On a previous visit to Edinburgh with James, I had severely criticised the housekeeping. Fran was keen to make amends.. The shops had been transformed. Fran started his working career with us and had then spent ten years with Automagic. He, too, wanted to talk about upside-down management. "It's weird at first," he observed, "but it works. It brings a very relaxed attitude and proves you don't need strict discipline. Although you allow people to do what they want, all Timpson shops look the same and our housekeeping is better than other shoe repairers."

In Kirkcaldy our day finished on a positive note. I talked with Alan Milne, who has run shops in Edinburgh, Inverness and Dunfermline before going to Kirkcaldy five years ago.

"You met my son earlier today," he said.

"Yes," I replied, "he was in St James' Centre, Edinburgh, learning to sew a welt."

"I have another son waiting to work for you," continued Alan, "but as he is only 13 he will join as an apprentice in 2011."

Employees who recruit their own children pay us a very high compliment. Conversations like that keep a 65-year-old working full-time. (I do need the odd pat on the back to keep me going.)

THAMES VALLEY

The feedback had been pretty positive so far but I needed to talk to someone with the reputation for being blunt – Perry Watkins. I chatted to Perry during one day when we visited 13 shops between Swindon and Reading.

Perry is only too happy to speak his mind. He joined the business in 1980 when we bought W H Broughall and he was running its shop in Aylesbury. He was a scruffy young man with a moustache and long hair. Few would have predicted that he would become our associate director, sales, with 630 branches under his wing.

He surprised me by starting on a positive note. "I like the way we develop new projects," he said. "We gradually spread ideas through the business by building up confidence. It's not a question of tablets of stone being handed down by senior management. It is more a consensus that only lets us pursue things that create success. Although someone decides on the final plan, no big boss takes the credit. People know that the company belongs to you and James but they make decisions as if it were their own money. It's in sharp contrast to those companies where people protect their power base and pursue promotion. They push their own decisions at the expense of the corporate good."

I was in for some deep thinking as Perry continued in this serious vein for most of the day. "If you want to understand what makes Timpson different, talk to people who joined us from another company. Minit and Automagic area managers struggled with upside-down management. That's not surprising because our own area managers found it difficult at first. It's not easy to let your team have so much freedom. The managers who survived were willing to learn how to truly delegate. I soon saw the advantage," said Perry. "It makes a big difference when the people who really know about the detail – those who serve customers – have their say and help with the important decisions. Other retailers think head office has the right to decide everything. As a result, they are inflexible."

I had prepared Perry for this conversation; it was clear he had given it a lot of thought. "The balance of power is vital," he said. "I want the people in our shops to have a major say. They can tell you so much more than figures produced at head office."

We had been talking for two hours and visited four shops before Perry introduced a hint of criticism. "I worry about schemes to save money," he said. "It's fine if no one notices. That means we have cut expenditure that the business didn't need. But in Timpson it is tempting to save money by cutting out things we would really miss.

"In the early 1990s, the firm was going through a sticky time. Shoe repairs were dropping like a stone and we were all very worried. I remember that at an area managers' conference, during a particularly poor period of trading, you said that you were going to double the training budget rather than cut it because that was the way to secure our future. That made a big impression on me. Although I applaud cost-consciousness, I worry that money will be saved by eliminating some of our vital ingredients – such as training, the size of our area management team and the generosity of the Timpson bonus.

"We have found success by being different from others. When business is bad, we have the common sense to keep spending money on the magic dust that makes our business special. A conventional executive would cut costs and so commit some of our vital heritage to history."

"In most companies the big decisions are discussed and decided by head office. Thankfully, at Timpson the debate takes place in the field. Customers and shop staff have their say, and our executives take note of their views."

We were approaching the centre of Oxford but there was no stopping Perry. "My worry about cost cutting increases the bigger the company gets. It is tempting to multiply savings by the number of shops, areas or employees. A ten per cent cut in head count is a big number. It would produce a huge and immediate impact on profits but, if the decision-makers are detached from our shops, they could cut out the secret of our success. No big decisions should be made until the decision-maker has spent a full week visiting shops to find out what is happening and what people think. The bigger we get, the harder it is to keep in touch. It becomes more important to abandon the office and visit shops. It's good to be mean but sometimes saving money can be foolish."

As Perry spoke, I was thinking how lucky he was to work for a private company that doesn't have to produce quarterly results for analysts and institutional shareholders.

Perry switched the subject to marketing. "I am not a fan of market research and clever slogans," he said, "but our shops need more creativity. Marketing needs the input and support of shop staff to ensure success. They must approve of each promotion as much as they did when we launched our new Rhino sole with its lifetime guarantee. You didn't get the same support when we cut the cost and quality of key blanks by substituting steel for brass."

No one is more aware of our achievements than Perry but, he warned, "great results are not necessarily a cause for constant rejoicing. We must not fall in love with our success story. Is upside-down management working as well as we think? We have gone much further than most companies but I wonder how many area managers delegate as far as we want? From my observation, area teams don't always let go. Many shop staff ignore the freedom they have been given. It's human nature; some people like being told what to do but still resent the rules about wearing ties and not using radios. They know why these rules are important, but they still don't respect them."

As we approached Reading, Perry showed his true pessimism. "The business will always live on a tightrope," he said. "It wouldn't take long for the magic dust to disappear. We must maintain the quality of our raw materials and constantly search for new ideas. As soon as we stop finding ways to increase the branch bonus, we will lose the support and respect of the people who matter most – the people who serve our customers."

THE MIDLANDS

Perry had given me plenty to think about. His observation – that people with experience of other businesses had a different perspective and were in a better position to judge where we succeed and where we fail – was confirmed when I visited the Midlands the following week.

Paul Masters, the manager at the larger of our two shops in Coventry, had spent several years at Minit. I asked him about our paperwork. "When you threw out the EPOS system it gave us the right message," he said. "We were back in charge of the shops and ex-Minit people started to realise you were going to make a difference."

I always enjoy visiting Stratford, where we have a small branch with a big turnover. The shop was full of customers when I arrived. I tried to help a middle-aged lady look for long leather laces. When the shop quietened down, I went into the basement with the manager Dick Bujnicki to look at the figures. Dick had fallen in love with our bonus. "But you have got to be hungry," he said. "Some people lack the drive to enjoy the bonus."

YORKSHIRE

Later that week I paid my first visit to our new shop in Pontefract. I had been to the town nine months earlier when the site was on offer (James and I try to visit every proposed site before making a final decision). The shop was run by Andy Ball, who had spent many years with Minit. He used a Yorkshire expression to describe working for Timpson. "It's about getting tret," he said. "You get backing and you can do what you want. For a few years I worked for Somerfield. But they were so formal. Life here is much more relaxed."

Perry was right. It was good to get an outsider's view.

The following week I made another trip to Scotland. It was a long day, starting from my home in Cheshire to Dumfries, through Ayr and Greenock before finishing at Helensburgh. I misjudged the traffic and it was well past closing time when I met Ian Gallagher, a mobile manager who had been looking after the shop for six weeks. Ian started in the trade at 16 with an independent shoe repairer in Partick. He spent five years in an old-style workshop where he never served a customer. He has a broad Scottish accent but I hadn't the courage to ask him to speak slowly. Instead I listened very carefully.

He was keen to show me the figures. Before he arrived, the daily takings were £250; now he is disappointed with £450. "I can't imagine what they were doing," he said. "Perhaps they kept the door shut and sat in the back reading a newspaper." It never ceases to amaze me that one person can make a massive overnight difference to a shop's turnover.

Ian had been given a trial in Stirling by Brian McKeown, an ambitious Timpson employee who left to build up a chain called Uppermost. Within two years, Ian had been named salesman of the year. After five years he left to run his own taxi company but, later, the Uppermost area manager persuaded him to return. Ian had been working for Uppermost when we bought the business.

Uppermost had been one of our stronger competitors and Brian McKeown knew the game. I was interested to hear how Ian compared the two companies. "At Uppermost," said Ian, "you only saw Brian if you were doing badly. I met him about once a year. Now, if I have a problem my area manager sorts it out and gives me as much time as I need. My regional manager, Alex Barrett, also shows a real interest – he always asks after my wife and two kids.

"Their bonus scheme was similar but different people got different targets, which I thought was unfair. There was little training. We introduced watch repairs but never got further than fitting straps and batteries. Brian kept his prices down – he thought Timpson was too expensive. He tried to make staff wear ties but eventually that lapsed. He let his staff wear trainers. I'm glad you realise uniform is so important."

I interrupted him. "I can never understand why our people take off their tie to walk 30 yards to buy their lunch. Some even change into trainers."

Ian looked a little irritated that I had stopped him in full flow. "There is another thing. Brian didn't like paying out for complaints. At Timpson, you spend more money on your shops and it makes a difference. Even the non-refitted branches are better than Brian's best."

Ian had written a list in readiness for my arrival. "Your bonus scheme makes a big difference. We definitely get more freedom, but it is the training that sets you apart. The training courses are brilliant. They give you a chance to meet up with the rest of the guys. The first time I ever saw other people from Uppermost was when I joined Timpson."

"So I have no complaints," said Ian, summing up. "I like the birthdays off and love the idea of the holiday homes. The way I see it, you run the business by helping us to make you the money."

Three months after this conversation, Ian left us to open a shop of his own. I respect him for having the courage to start his own business. And if it doesn't work out, he will be welcome back.

TIMPSON HOUSE

I had talked to a lot of people in the shops. It was time to get a view from Timpson House. I arranged to meet Karina Kenna, who started with Timpson 28 years ago. She is a member of a small group of women in our finance department who all joined us at around the same time. Today they occupy key positions in our day-to-day administration and have become firm friends outside work. At times, I think Karina knows the business better than I do. She must be one of the best unqualified accountants in the country, with an instinct for spotting where figures are wrong and a genius for giving me exactly the information I need. I rate Karina very highly and so she was an ideal person to tell me not only about the reasons for our success but also our shortcomings.

"When I started," said Karina, "the office bell went at 9.00am and again at 5.00pm. You were Mr John and I worked for Mr Abbott and Mr Cookson. I knew I had made progress when I was asked to make the chief accountant's coffee. I am still here mainly because I like the people I work with and I'm allowed to be me. I am kept informed and, most of all, feel I have played a part in making this business what it is. It works two ways. I feel valued by the business and in turn I know my people rely on me. If I am ever unhappy, I know I can talk about it. I have always found it easy to discuss problems with you and feel the same about James. Not many people have the courage to knock on the boss's door, even if it is Richard Branson. I admire your honest, straightforward approach. You don't give us any bullshit."

I interrupted her. "Thanks, Karina," I said, "but are you typical of the average Timpson House employee?" She looked slightly irritated. I had stopped her chain of thought. "If anyone doesn't like the way the company is run," she replied, "they might as well go elsewhere. We are unlikely to change. It is a family business run by the same people year after year.

"But I have seen a big change in the past ten years. You do a lot more to look after us, with benefits such as the Hardship Fund, holiday homes and more training. In five years I have had much more training than in the previous 20.

"I like the way we are forward-thinking. I never thought our cobblers would repair watches. We now have laptops for area managers. Even the chairman has a BlackBerry," said Karina, and she gave me a slightly sarcastic smile.

"You don't make decisions in an ivory tower. You listen to what people say. It is refreshing to see us revisit decisions. If it doesn't work, we change it. Even if it does work, you still ask 'can it be done better?'"

It was a vote of confidence from Karina but I wanted her view on Timpson House. "I want Timpson House to be the ultimate helpline," I said. "How are we doing?"

"I wish I had spent more time visiting branches," she replied. "My department doesn't make money. We just count it. People in the branches make the profit. If we are not careful, head office decisions get in the way. Sometimes I think we should know the area managers better. I would like to see more of them poking their noses into the finance department."

"I like the freedom of upside-down management but we still need office discipline," she continued. "We can't allow bad habits like lateness affect business. Personality makes a big difference. Superstars save money because with great people you don't need as big a team to do the work. I want stars like Sharon Fleury, who looks after stocktaking but will turn her mind to anything. She provides 110 per cent when others would struggle.

"It makes a big difference working with conscientious people. People flexible enough to pick up a ringing phone that is not their own, then take a message and follow everything through to a conclusion."

I interrupted again. "Does that mean we need more superstars?"

"Some people here don't appreciate how good the business is," Karina replied. "You must be able to see what needs to be done without being told. Louise Appleby, in my department, came from Cauldwell Communications, which was a successful but tough environment. Louise loves it here because she doesn't have to stay until 10pm or save paper by writing on the back of old memos. Stupid penny-pinching is a pain. Once, during an economy drive, we ran out of paper in the mail room and couldn't send out the newsletter.

"I like the benefits you give. Pensions are less appreciated but probably the most important. Young people don't think about old age but, when they reach mid-career and compare our deal with other companies, they will appreciate what the company is doing.

"For most of my career, Timpson House training has been pretty pathetic, but the recent coaching has helped me become a better manager and made me think. I now realise the importance of looking after my people's well-being; it is a real challenge.

"We are no different from anywhere else when it comes to rumours, but we communicate much more than ten years ago and it makes a difference. So please continue with the area conferences, James's monthly Town Hall meeting and the weekly newsletter. I don't always read it," she added, "but I know it is there to tell me what is going on.

"I have visited enough companies to know that most other purchase ledger departments don't do it in the way we do. I want us to keep it that way, so please don't allow standardisation to be stamped on us."

Karina was also pleased about the weeding out of "drongos".

"Over the years," she said, "I have recognised the signs of an office drongo. They arrive after 9am and leave bang on 5pm. They walk past a ringing phone and ignore litter lying on the floor. They have no appetite for work but claim there is a morale problem. They don't ask 'what can I do next?', 'can I give a hand?' or 'do you want me to stay late?' They simply do their job – nothing more, nothing less.

"You have considerably improved our canteen but drongos still whinge about the size of portions and the crispness of the bacon.

"We have better people now than ever before but they need more training. With such a brilliant training scheme in the branches, why don't we do the same for Timpson House? Head office people should know more about our business. Teach them how to step back and let their team get on with it.

"In the end, I suppose," said Karina, looking me straight in the eye, "I work for you. Please keep caring for the business as it really matters to me."

EAST ANGLIA

In Ipswich the following week, I was brought down to earth. It was at the beginning of what promised to be a long day: Ipswich, Lowestoft, Norwich, Kings Lynn, and then home to Cheshire – seven shop visits and about 250 miles.

Keith Winter, one of our Ipswich managers, is an ex-Minit man. When

I asked him what he thought of Timpson I expected the enthusiasm shown by other ex-Minit employees. "Minit was better," he said, after a little reflection. "They told us what to do and I didn't have to think about it. I don't like taking skill tests," he said. "I never liked exams, so your training scheme has been difficult." I was disappointed at his response. It showed that our way of doing business doesn't work with everybody. "I was working in the Sainsbury's concession when you took over," Keith said. "It was a Minit Solutions, the concept Minit had introduced after buying Sketchley and SupaSnaps. It didn't work with Minit and you didn't make it any better."

I reached home at 8.30pm, tired and a tiny bit depressed. But, in two days' time, Alex and I would be in Mustique, our favourite island in the Caribbean. There I relax, play a bit of tennis, drink the odd rum punch, read a few books, and – apart from the occasional glance at my BlackBerry – forget about the business.

Chapter 6
WHAT OUR PEOPLE SAY (Part 2)

My Mustique holiday was great. Years ago, my holiday feeling wore off very quickly. Within hours of returning to the office I was stressed out by the pile of post and backlog of work; today I am better organised. My BlackBerry helps, providing a constant update from base that ensures there are no surprises awaiting my return. Before I go away I make a list of all the current projects and major issues to help me pick up the plot on my return. But I don't rush straight in; the first day back is spent in gossip, talking to colleagues to catch up with news I have missed. Although my tour was a top priority item, it was a week before I got out my A4 pad again.

TIMPSON HOUSE

It was time to speak to a relative newcomer. Paresh Majithia, our finance director, joined us in January 2004 with experience gained at Woolworths, Asda and UCI. It can't have been easy to enter a family company and work so closely with father and son.

Paresh arrived when we had been turned upside-down by the take-over of Minit. Rapid change plus many more shops rocked the normal stability of our finance department. We hadn't lost control of the numbers but we were getting pretty close; the burden of a £5m overdraft created considerable unease. Four years later we are back in the black and the finance department is firmly in control. Father and son have a great respect for what Paresh is doing. He has played a major part in the boardroom since his arrival.

I asked Paresh to tell me his first impressions. "I find it difficult to describe to other people," he started, "but it is definitely different at Timpson. You allow people to get on with it. As James said: 'If you can take more money by painting shops pink, that's fine by me.' Our management team is almost entirely home-grown but you have trained them to be real experts. Instead of having loads of KPIs as some companies do, you keep the targets simple: daily cash, weekly turnover and monthly profit. Communication is better than in a lot of businesses; producing a company newsletter week after week for many years must have a huge impact.

"Despite a long period of success," continued Paresh, "you still have the ability to change your mind. I don't find people making excuses or covering their backs. Our flexibility is worth a lot. It is different being part of a private business that takes a long-term view.

"Without market research you have an amazing knowledge of the market. The experience you and James have of the high street is invaluable. I wonder how many other retail executives with more than 550 shops know them so well and visit them so regularly."

PHILIP WHITMORE'S EMAIL

Straight after talking to Paresh, I received a copy of an email sent to James from Philip Whitmore. Here's what it said:

"Sorry to bother you. I know how busy you are but feel that after what I have gone through you should be made aware how good some of your field staff are. I was managing the shop in Piccadilly, Manchester, and after one too many awkward customers decided enough was enough and found another job.

"Darren Brown, my area manager, told me I was a valued member of staff and that I would always be welcomed back. His ADM, Steve Melville, kept in touch, often ringing to tell me how much I was missed, but neither of them tried to discourage me in my effort to better myself (that's what I thought I was doing). But it wasn't the dream job I expected and when I finally saw sense and asked to be reinstated both Darren and Steve were very helpful.

"I actually feel like I never left. I made a stupid mistake. In a strange way I feel ashamed I turned my back on Timpson. Darren Brown has treated me so well I thought it should be noted just how well a people person he is. He has done nothing but support me through my moment of stupidity and he has guided me back to the job I love and enjoy with the help of Steve Melville.

"I sent a text message to Darren, thanking him for his help but feel recognition is best delivered by someone like yourself. If I was to get a pat on the back from the top I know it would mean an awful lot. They are a credit to the company and by far the best area team I have worked for in 21 years in the shoe repair trade.

"Kindest regards, your now loyal employee Philip Whitmore, Manager 831 Swinton from Monday morning."

THE NORTH-WEST

So the next person to talk to was Darren Brown. Darren has been an area manager for four years and lives near Blackpool, where we gave him his training as a lad more than 25 years ago. He is consistently rated highly by his team. I hoped he would reveal how to develop such excellent management. I met Darren at our shop in Lytham St Anne's and we went four doors down the street to Caffè Nero.

"I don't start with the wage statistics," said Darren. "I look at the people. They should be happy at work; if they are grumpy, I've got a problem. Making positive personalities work alongside someone with little to offer is a hammer blow to morale. To create the right atmosphere you must lose the people that we all call drongos.

"I look at staffing from the branch point of view. I want them to have fun, grow the turnover and earn a big bonus. It is a question of putting yourself in their position.

"The benefits we provide are very important. I like what we do for birthdays. Families like the fact we send a card; colleagues really appreciate getting their birthday off. I appreciate our pension scheme but not everyone sees the value. We need to sell its benefits much more as they are as good as anything on the market. I am particularly keen to make sure the holiday homes are allocated to people who really deserve them.

"Take Fred Harrison, who works in Manchester. He hadn't been away for years, so I drove him and his wife to our holiday home at Ribby Hall, took them out for a Chinese meal on the Wednesday night and dropped them back home at the end of their stay. That really showed we cared."

Darren was now in full flight. I bought him another coffee. "In other companies, staff stand to attention when their area manager arrives. That is not my way. My area team talks to everyone as equals. That builds trust and loyalty. "You and James treat me as if we are on the same level," he added. "I like that, so I do the same to everyone in my area."

Good colleagues give good customer care and it is our job to look after them," Darren continued, "and not just in work but outside. I have two football teams: one has been promoted to their league premiership; the other doesn't have great footballers but they enjoy meeting up for a kick around."

"Before I was an area manager," said Darren, sipping at his coffee, "plenty of other people have managed me. One area manager had absolutely no personality and could not communicate. As a result, we spent too much time on the phone complaining about him and spreading rumours.

"The area manager must press the right buttons. That means putting the right people in the right shops. When we were under-performing in Cross Street, Manchester, I spent a day in the branch and the problem became obvious. We had two good guys desperate to take money and earn their bonus but the third guy spent the day reading his paper. We replaced him with Freda, who always gives 100 per cent, and the atmosphere changed and turnover shot up.

"Branch colleagues will watch their area manager very closely. If he makes them buy cheap Hoovers and sack the window cleaner, they will think he is saving costs simply to increase his own bonus at their expense. Before long he will lose respect.

"My secret is to have a great area team. I have three ADMs and four mobiles who are given freedom to do anything anyone else does. So there is me and a team of seven, all helping our branches to do better. We need to keep our own skills and customer care up to date and be as good as the people in our branches. The trick is to know the detail but then stand back and take a bird's eye view of the area.

Darren then moved onto a pet topic – the bonus. "We always need to think about it," he said. "It is the best thing we have ever invented. In Salford, we reduced the staffing level from four down to two but increased our turnover. It's amazing. The bigger the bonus, the better the buzz in the shop. Customers really notice it."

It was interesting to hear Darren's comments on how he, himself, was being managed. "I get on with Alex Barrett, my regional manager," he replied, "as he tells you the truth. Although he is not on the phone every day, I always feel he is there for me. In fact, the whole management team is there to give advice.

"I organise my area so that if I was ever away for three months it would still run okay. Recently I helped to run the company time management course. Another area manager asked me how I could fit it in. He found it difficult to create the two free days just to come on the course." It amused Darren – somebody not being able find the time to go on a time management course.

"Of all the services we provide," I asked Darren, "what matters most?"

"The main thing is customer care," Darren replied. "The DVDs taken by our mystery shoppers simply can't lie. People like to see the truth about themselves, so seeing it on camera is a real revelation. We must keep pushing the customer care message. I've got some great salesmen. My star is Steve Manley; I wish I had 20 Steves.

"Sometimes we underestimate the importance of loyalty. Some people have been critical of Minit but that acquisition brought us some excellent staff. These are people who are naturally loyal and don't like change – that's why they stuck with Minit through thick and thin. That loyalty is a great quality which we can use to our advantage."

I felt I knew Darren well enough to ask my next question.

"What do you think of my role?" I asked.

"I often think about that," said Darren. "I wonder whether the guy who runs Boots visits every shop like you do. The other week I was in Morecambe. When I arrived, James was there talking to Carla, the manager, about her planned holiday to Malaysia. He wasn't just making small talk. He was really interested and, when he got back to the office, sent her a travel book to take on her journey.

"We like the interest you take in our shops. We like the fact you are always looking for the next idea. Other businesses seem to wait until sales drop ten per cent before they panic into action. With us, something new comes along every few months and that keeps the business moving forward. Without that, we wouldn't be doing watch repairs or be so big into training."

"So, Darren," I interrupted, "tell me more about training, as I feel that is the best way to improve our business."

"You are right," replied Darren, "but training is a never-ending job. Older people with more than 20 years' service are the hardest to get switched on about it but we are getting there. Talented people want to move up the ladder. When I started, you had to wait ten years before you got a shop. Now it depends how good you are."

"But all these wonderful ideas," added Darren, looking more serious, "don't work with the drongos. They resist change. They are scared of skill tests. I am very happy to pay the good people well and look after them. But if someone can't be bothered, I am quick to say goodbye.

Losing a drongo was a big problem. We used to put the poorest people on relief. Even now, some area managers hide them in big shops. That irritates the good people and ruins their bonus. Good people hate drongos. My job is to look after the good people, so I must make sure the drongos work for someone else.

"I had a guy recently who was paying into the Child Support Agency. The maximum he could earn each week for himself was £180. Everything else went to the CSA. The bonus made no difference. The only way he could increase his take-home pay was to pinch money from the till. And that's what he did.

"But there are plenty of people with the right attitude. Alex, who joined us at Blackpool, took an £80 cut in his basic pay compared with his dead-end job in a plastic bag factory. He made up the difference with his bonus. He is happy because he is now treated like a human being.

"As I said at the beginning, it is about the way you treat people. You must be reliable. If I promise to do a simple thing like getting the warehouse to send a new shirt, I have got to make sure it is done. If you let people down, they will let you down in return.

"It is all a question of how I treat my people and of how you treat me. It is nice to see new people joining the business with the same attitude. I feel I can walk into the office at Wythenshawe and talk to anyone. Last time I was there, Paresh asked me into his office for a chat and a cup of coffee. I wonder how many other finance directors know their area managers well enough to do that."

SCOTLAND

Darren had a lot of praise for his regional manager, Alex Barrett. So I wanted to meet Alex on his home ground, which meant a trip to Glasgow.

On the way, I stopped at Galashiels. It's always a pleasure to visit this border town, where Jim Gow has been manager for 16 years. He talked about the "them and us" feeling of the old days. "Thank goodness we don't have to suffer in silence any more," he said. "I can talk to Alex and Andy, my area manager. If I've got a problem, they will listen."

"When I talk to friends about my job they can't believe we have holiday homes and birthdays off. Some years I'm allowed four weeks holiday to visit my family in South Africa. My friends are not just jealous of the perks; the pay is pretty good, too, because of the bonus scheme. Please promise you will never change the way we do the bonus."

A few weeks earlier I had talked to Brian Low, our manager in the Trinity Centre, Aberdeen. He had told me a story about Alex Barrett. "Last year," Brian had said, "Alex promised that if I beat my sales target for the year he would get me tickets to Old Trafford. I beat the target and he kept his word."

I was able to copy Alex's example later that day when I met John Kelly at East Kilbride. John told me he would love to see my team Manchester City play Chelsea. "Because," he said, with a note of apology, "my son is a Chelsea supporter." I phoned Christine in the office to arrange the tickets. Within 15 minutes it was done.

Before meeting Alex, I called at Greenock. Sammy, who now runs a shop there, is one of many good musicians in our business. In fact, Sammy is so good that he once left for five years to tour with his band in Europe. Although he now misses the music, he is glad to be back. His biggest respect is reserved for his colleagues: "I like the fact we are all grafters," he told me.

Alex Barrett started as an apprentice 25 years ago. I first remember him as the manager of our Asda concession in Coatbridge, shortly before becoming one of our few franchisees with a shop in Kilmarnock. Alex speaks broad Glaswegian at the speed of an express train. He is full of common sense. We sat down in the Asda café in Parkhead, just south-east of Glasgow's city centre. It isn't comfortable but it is conveniently situated near one of our shops and the car park is free. Once Alex began to talk, I soon forgot about the surroundings.

"We've changed even faster than the world around us," was Alex's opening observation. "The business is so much more complicated. I was terrified of my area manager but in those days we did as we were told. I was a bit of a rebel. One day, my boss got so annoyed with me he ripped the phone of the wall at Coatbridge. I upset him so much he had to take a day off to recover his composure.

"We all had to follow rigid guidelines. It took four people to take £1,000 in a week. Bill Taylor made a big difference when he became our area manager. He was much more approachable. He told us the truth and listened to our opinion. We had never had that freedom before.

"When I became an area manager, I simply aimed to get the right team in every branch and then go round to talk to them. I wanted to see if anything was stopping them taking money. I was always careful never to make false promises.

"I try to carry out my regional role in the same way. I'm helped by a great set of area managers. You would not believe their loyalty. If you cut Rab Mitchell's arm off, he would be bleeding Timpson." (Rab looks after Ireland.)

A waitress hovered round, hoping to clear the table. One look from Alex was enough to send her away. "Today," Alex continued, "area managers are wary of treating people in the wrong way and being criticised by personnel. In the old days, we took them out the back and told them the facts of life in blunt language. There was no messing about. Now Gouy, our people support director, tells every employee their rights. It makes things more difficult. All this employment legislation is part of a politically correct world. I can see the point of it, but for the good of the business we have to find a way round it.

"Good people should get the praise and support they need. Drongos should get the sack. The more drongos we have in the business, the worse we will do. The best area managers are good at spotting them."

"Area managers find it difficult to deal with problem people if they are short of staff. We must always aim to have a waiting list. We need to have a substitute bench ready to replace the drongos. Recently, we made a major step forward by changing the role of the roving manager. We used to have relief managers who were often the worst people in the business. Now, thank goodness, we have developed the concept of the mobile manager. The best people are now our mobiles."

"Although we talk a lot about drongos, we have a lot of really good managers. One of my greatest pleasures is giving them a pat on the back."

Alex paused for breath, so I took the chance to alter his train of thought.

"Where do we need to improve?" I asked.

"We have a big gap," said Alex. "There are not enough women in this company. No area team has found a place for a woman. That's got to change for the good of the business. We have got to make better use of our female talent.

"I welcome the benefits and I'm particularly keen on the hardship fund and the holiday homes. But we must make sure we look after the good people. Don't send drongos on free holiday breaks."

"You have made things difficult for yourself," he said, looking me straight in the eye. "Our people now expect to be well looked after. They have heard so much about Timpson being a great place to work. If they do a good job, they expect to be recognised. Make sure the biggest perks go to the people who really deserve them."

"Sometimes," said Alex, giving me another severe Scottish stare, "you don't realise how many things an area team has to do. We need to help the area teams get their priorities right and make sure training is at the top of their list.

"I worry that training can take a back seat. The biggest benefit comes when we train people on customer care. The recent mystery shopper DVDs have been wonderful. The more emphasis we put on mystery shopping, the better our service will become."

We had finished our coffees. The waitress was hovering again. I asked Alex one final question: "What's your biggest fear for the future?"

"Having enough staff," he said. "Don't copy those cost-cutting exercises I see in other businesses. Don't cut staff levels too far. You always need someone waiting in the wings ready to take over when the next drongo has to leave."

HAMPSHIRE

I usually visit shops on my own but sometimes I meet up with a member of the area team. I spent one morning with Simon Childs, who had only recently been appointed area manager. When I met him at our shop in Fleet at 8.45am, he looked pretty nervous. He had been there very early and his suit looked new. He soon seemed to forget he was with the chairman and began to exude enthusiasm for his new job.

"You need to be confident to get their confidence," he said to me. "Lots of bosses rely on rules because they themselves are insecure. Your upside-down management isn't for wimps. It is for managers who have the courage to give people freedom.

"You can't delegate if you have doubts about your own ability. I've got a big advantage as everyone knows that I know what I'm talking about. After all, only a few months ago I was doing their job. I work most Saturdays as it keeps my hand in."

I asked him if there was anything I could do to help him.

"Not really," he replied. "Just as long as someone is at the end of the phone and willing to help if I have a problem, that's all I need."

WALES

I often reflect how lucky we are to have so many enthusiastic managers. I found another when I visited St Mary Street in Cardiff. Eric Sysum had plenty of praise for his area team.

"If I've got a problem, I can always get help from Gareth Drewe and his ADMs. They have just given me something really good to look forward to – the chance to run our new watch repair shop in Salisbury. That's what I call a real busman's holiday. I can't wait to show everyone what I can do." And show us he did. In his first week Eric nearly doubled the shop's turnover.

TIMPSON HOUSE

By now I had filled lots of A4 pads. But I wanted one more meeting at Timpson House. I arranged an hour with Rosemary Whitehead. She looks after our pension fund which, due to her determination, is one of those rare gems – a final salary scheme that is still open to new members.

"I started as a part-timer in 1985," Rosemary began, "and worked for several other companies while I was working for Timpson. There was a stark contrast between your business and some others. I got a different feeling at Timpson. I felt I was coming home here. This was the place I wanted to be. You're not playing a game. It is run properly and you do things properly.

"It made a difference when you sold the shoe shops because you got rid of the other shareholders and could do what you wanted. You were allowed to develop your own style. I understand why your wife Alex told you not to float the company. She was dead right. Institutional shareholders are not for you."

Listening to Rosemary, I began to realise how much she must have studied the way I go about my job.

"Twenty years ago," she continued, "you stopped doing what everyone else did. Instead of following the herd, you made your own judgments using common sense.

"The takeover of Minit was a revelation. It was a business full of admin folk. Compared to them, we're almost a one-man band. They had a big, costly infrastructure but didn't know what was going on in their shops.

"There is a good ambiance in Timpson House. It is a good place to work, even if some people could get more pay elsewhere. I don't feel I have to work late. The company makes sensible decisions, such as your view about pensions.

"But one thing worries me. If you and James weren't here, it would not be the same. I accept that getting bigger is necessary. But we must retain our style. It would be a disaster to be a target-driven company run by a committee that takes away our freedom. I want you to keep it simple. When you visit branches or come round the office, you make people feel they are worthwhile. It is good that you talk to us. I have enjoyed our talk this morning.

"The business is like a family. I feel like a member of that family. I read the history. Your grandfather invented something special with his shop visits and hand-written notes. Don't change the way you do it. Please don't let standards drop. Keep hounding the area managers about poor performing shops and drongos. Never cut down on training or reduce the size of our area teams. Keep giving people the freedom but watch them carefully. And keep talking to us because, as long as you keep the business as relaxed as it is now, we will never be frightened to tell you if there is a problem."

"You have told me a lot in the past hour," I said to Rosemary. "How would you sum it all up?"

"Lots of things have made this a good business," she replied. "We need you and James to make sure we stick to the principles that created our success. In case we all forget, please write everything down. We need to remember the things that make this such a great place to work."

I had talked enough. Rosemary was right. The time had come to write it all down.

I had been told lots of things. They gave me some consistent messages. They want our business to keep changing but they don't want to change the way we run it. They want us to keep it simple and avoid acting like a big business.

Some pointed to special features that they felt really made a difference. But, whoever they were and whatever their view, the biggest fear is that we will, over time, get swallowed up by professional business practice and, in the process, lose the magic dust that has created such a fascinating business.

I'm glad my father taught me to visit shops. It's the part of my job that has provided me with the most pleasure. The weeks going round with my A4 pad produced an added bonus – I had never had such frank conversations about our culture. For the first time, people were telling me what they thought about the way we run the business.

I'm sure they would all agree with Rosemary when she told me to write it all down. That's what this book tries to do. I hope it will help protect Timpson from the dangers of progress and serve as a constant reminder of the magic dust that has created a successful culture.

Chapter 7

ONLY GREAT PEOPLE NEED APPLY

“Personality makes a big difference – superstars save us money ” Karina Kenna

It made a great difference when we stopped recruiting cobblers and picked people on personality. Before, it seemed sensible to look for shoe repair and key cutting experts. In retrospect, we were dramatically limiting our choice. There were only 30,000 people in the UK with the right qualifications.

Life-long cobblers said it would take five years to teach a raw recruit to repair a quality shoe. We proved them wrong. We turned positive personalities into good craftsmen within 12 months. We have never found a way to turn a grumpy cobbler into a positive personality.

Many years ago I invited Dean Butler, the founder of Vision Express, to talk to a group of our area managers. It was when our business was one-third of the size it is now. The area managers' meeting took place in the dining room of our home in Cheshire. Dean talked about his experience in Canada, where he had expanded his business to saturation point. "Up to then," he said, "my main aim was to grow the company. But the next year I set a different target: I sought to have a good manager in every branch. All other KPIs were put on hold. My executive team replaced weak managers with superstars. As a result, the company produced record profits by some distance."

After the conference ended, Kit Green, our managing director, talked to me. "That's fine," he said, "but what is the sign of a superstar?" "That's easy," I replied. "Good managers take the most money."

In every business good managers make a difference. In Timpson, the difference is dramatic. Whenever we change a manager, turnover goes up or down.

In 2005 we opened a new shop in Villiers Street, London. It's a busy spot between Embankment and the head office of PricewaterhouseCoopers. After the first few months, sales settled at a weekly average of £1,400 – woefully below expectations. We changed the management. Within two weeks, turnover had reached £3,000.

Across our business we have successes and failures. It is the people that almost always make the difference. For 20 years I have heard the same excuses: "no one comes to town since they altered the one-way streets"; "everything has changed since Tesco moved out of town"; "now they charge for car parking, everyone goes to [insert name of nearest other town here]"; and the popular "all traders are complaining everyone is quiet round here".

Occasionally there is a genuine excuse, such as when the Meadowhall Shopping Centre was flooded, or when our street in Folkestone was closed for building work. But if the cause of the problem is unclear, assume it is to do with people. Ninety per cent of excuses disappear with a good manager.

This chapter has a simple message: good people make a big difference. They do much more than increase sales. They are great to work with and inspire others. They create the buzz in the business. In the process, they produce ideas for the future. Good people are the custodians of your culture.

Superstars are a great asset not just because they produce more profit but they also make the business fun. My greatest enjoyment is meeting buzzy superstars such as PJ, who runs our branch in Union Arcade, Reading – a place that locals call "smelly alley". With his infectiously cheerful personality, PJ has made his shop a happy oasis on a miserable high street.

Stuart Williams in Witney is more serious but certainly knows how to take money. He was our first person to realise the potential of passport photos. Through his own initiative, he grew weekly sales to £250 and this inspired us to spread the service throughout the company.

We have also learned a lot from Divna, who looks after our watch repair service in Selfridges. We thought that £500 was a good weekly watch repair turnover until we met Divna – she does £5,000. We have decided to develop a separate watch repair chain so I mentioned the idea to Divna. Her eyes lit up. She was keen to manage our first one in London.

"How could I find your replacement?" I said.

"I know your problem," she replied. "Most watch repairers can't talk to customers. If you can't sell, you don't take money. Find me the right personality and I'll teach them the job."

You learn a lot from good people. Adrian Jennison in Beverley has put his personality into his shop; everyone can see it in his displays, which include pictures of his staff nights out, complimentary letters and framed cuttings of Adrian's appearance in the local newspaper.

I want a business full of characters who use their initiative to make things happen. I am not inspired by people who stick to the rules. So let's go back to Kit Green's question: how do you define a good manager?

They are hard-working people who enjoy serving customers and love earning lots of money. Ask them to do something and they say "no problem". They don't look for excuses. They make life fun. Colleagues enjoy their company. They know exactly how much money they have taken today.

I want people who "get it" at every level – from senior manager to the new apprentice. They do exist. But we live in a world of equal opportunities, with employment legislation designed in the belief that everyone has the same potential. They do not. The population is divided into:

- five per cent – potential superstars
- 15 per cent – pretty good
- 40 per cent – average
- 25 per cent – poor
- 10 per cent – drongo
- five per cent – hopeless

We want the top 20 per cent. But there are not enough good people to go round. So our job is to employ the personalities and leave the rest to work for other companies.

So where do you find the personalities? We enlist the help of our workforce. Our "Introduce a friend" scheme gives £150 to anyone who introduces a recruit who remains with us for at least 16 weeks; another £250 is given once the recruit has completed a year. Forty-five per cent of new Timpson employees come to us through this scheme. It's why we have so many friends and relatives working in the business. Existing colleagues do the lion's share of our recruitment. They bring the best people because they introduce friends with similar personalities.

Good people attract more good people. With their reputation at stake, they are unlikely to land us with a duffer. Osman Isaaq came from Somalia and joined us as an apprentice in Barking. He was a superstar. He quickly rose to become manager at Canary Wharf before he left to run his own business. I asked Osman whether he had any brothers or sisters. "Yes," he said, "but none have the right attitude to work for this business."

Keep in touch with good employees who have left to work elsewhere. I don't resent people who try another career. It is often a sign of personality and determination. Good people are always welcome back. They often return with more experience and a better appreciation of what our company has to offer.

Good managers are always looking for talent. Alex Barrett found Rab Mitchell, our area manager in Ireland, at his local golf club. Jo Cooper, who manages our Staines shop, used to work for Brooks, a dry cleaning shop in Egham where we had a concession. She could see the way we ran our business and decided to join Timpson. It was a good move for both of us.

We don't advertise our shops. We rely on good service to create our image. The same approach should be used for recruitment. I would much rather attract applicants through a window poster than the Job Centre. Although we do find some superstars at the Job Centre, we have to interview plenty of applicants before we spot one.

Aim to interview every applicant – even when there is no job on offer. Every area manager should have a waiting list of good people at the end of the phone, ready to join us when the next vacancy occurs.

Interviewing is an art, not a science. Look for personality, not qualifications. Ask questions simply to get the candidate talking. The answers don't matter much. I learned a simple interview criteria from Claire Owen of the SG Group, who was a fellow speaker at a conference in London. Claire called it the lunch test. "I ask myself a simple question," Claire told me. "Would I be happy to lunch with this person?" If she can't envisage lasting through lunch, the interviewee hasn't the right personality to fit into her business. (When he was coaching the England rugby team, Sir Clive Woodward had a more severe test. He asked: "Could I fly across the Atlantic sitting next to this guy?")

We invented our own method to get interviewers to concentrate on personality. This is our Mr Men test. It's a series of little cartoons depicting Mr Keen, Mr Punctual, Mr Helpful, Mr Happy, Mr Dull, Mr Slow, Mr Late and Mrs Miserable (one woman to avoid sex discrimination). We ask the interviewer to tick the boxes that apply to the person before them. It's not scientific but it gets the message across.

We treat interviews as a two-way process. To attract the best recruits, the business has to be sold to them just as hard as they are selling their personality. Sometimes the interview doesn't last long. It's quite usual to make up your mind within five minutes. Drongos are quick to reveal their true self.

At a recent area meeting, we talked about some bizarre interviewees. One brought his mother who answered every question; another was wired for sound, only taking the earphone out of his left ear to hear the questions while still listening to his music.

However severe the staff shortage, we have learned never to take on an also-ran and not to rush even if we have found a superstar. We try to arrange a day's trial in one of our shops, because the opinion of the people they work with will be very useful. There should always be time for a second interview; after all, we are hopefully making an appointment for life. The interview continues after they start as an apprentice. Their progress is followed and we listen to other people's opinions. We check with their apprentice manager and find out how they perform on the two-day residential course that we run for new starters at Wythenshawe. If we have any doubts, the trial is ended and employment terminated. People who might just be okay are very seldom okay. The time and effort put into their training will almost certainly be wasted.

Whenever possible we promote from within. All 22 of our area managers started as apprentices. Many recruits join as teenagers with their personalities not yet perfectly formed. Maturity makes a big difference. Many will blossom – and it is our job to spot them. Potential superstars should have the chance to flourish, by being pushed up the organisation sooner than might be considered prudent. But they must not be given a challenge that you couldn't take on yourself. An impossible mission can destroy the confidence of potential stars, hamper their progress or, even worse, send them to a job elsewhere.

At every stage, we follow the Mr Men rules. We always pick people on personality. Even when we need to import specialist skills such as IT and finance, the Mr Men rules apply.

Of course, when filling a specialist post the CV does matter. But when they join Timpson we have to make sure they grasp the company culture and are converted to upside-down management.

We have never been tempted to recruit plastic professional managers with their business school training and buzzwords. Professional managers live in a world of business plans and key performance indicators. They follow "best practice", put in "proper processes" and reduce everything to fully-costed financial forecasts with no requirement for flair. This might work well in some organisations. It won't work with us. If one of these plastic people headed our business, they would ruin it within 12 months.

LESSONS

- Positive personalities create the buzz in our business
- Pick people on personality
- Always have a second interview
- If in doubt, end the trial period
- Promote "Introduce a Friend"
- Keep looking for talent – have a waiting list
- Ninety per cent of excuses disappear when you have a good manager
- Have a good manager in every branch
- Whenever possible promote from within
- With professional specialists – still recruit for personality

Chapter 8
A GREAT PLACE TO WORK

"You have made things difficult for yourself. Our people now expect to be well looked after" Alex Barrett

You might expect me to say that customers come first. Wrong. My top priority is looking after our colleagues, the people who look after our customers. If we create a great place to work, they will provide a great shopping experience.

A shoe repair shop isn't the most glamorous workplace. But my evidence shows that Timpson employees like it. We employ 1,800 people. In July 2007 we only had three vacancies for experienced staff. Most areas have a waiting list, with 150 people hoping that a vacancy will arise. Nearly 300 colleagues are related to someone else at Timpson; 24 per cent who leave the company ask for their job back. We must be doing something right.

For the past ten years, looking after employees has become an obsession that has paid dividends. Once someone becomes a Timpson employee, they have joined our club. We will give them something most companies don't offer: trust and support in times of difficulty.

We don't just see employees as a statistic. We meet them regularly. I expect every area manager to visit each of his branches every six weeks. James and I go to every branch as often as we can (usually every 18 months). We don't just visit the shop: we meet the people and talk to everyone while we are there. We trust them because we know them so well and watch them carefully.

It is important to support the mavericks – the people who have the courage to break rules and use their initiative to try out new ideas. It's these ideas that will help to shape our future. In most businesses, mavericks are told to toe the line. We encourage them to ignore the rules. People should be allowed to express their individuality. But we don't waste time on drongos who, unless you are careful, soak up time and prevent you from putting your effort into improving our superstars.

Praise people ten times as much as you criticise. There are loads of different ways to hand out praise – use as many as you can. Our trading week ends on a Thursday. On Friday, our area teams ring round every shop to find out the figures. Our IT department devised a scheme that would have done the job more cheaply but I wouldn't let them do it. The "ring round" is a vital part of each week's routine. It is not only an opportunity to discuss figures but provides the perfect chance to issue praise and talk about the week's events. They don't just discuss business, they also catch up on personal agendas: "has your wife recovered?", "did your son win the football match?", "have a good holiday".

Every good area manager has a stock of chocolates and wine in their car to hand out in recognition of a job well done.

I never send congratulations by email. The internet has put a premium on the hand-written letter. Personal praise is better spelt out in your own handwriting, addressed to the employee's home. I use a proper postage stamp and, to make that praise really welcome, enclose a cheque with the tax paid by the company. I send hand-written letters nearly every week to people who deserve a chairman's award.

Praise should never be routine. Once, when I visited PJ in Reading, he was beating his previous year's performance in the face of heavy price-cutting by a nearby competitor. During our conversation he mentioned his love of racing and that one of his ambitions was to go to Cheltenham. A few weeks later, I sent him two tickets for the festival.

Thankfully, this novel type of recognition is copied hundreds of times throughout the company. It is so commonplace I seldom hear the details. It was only by chance that I discovered that time when Alex Barrett fixed it for Brian Lowe, our manager in Trinity Centre, Aberdeen, to travel south and watch Manchester United play a vital match.

However sincere the praise, it is never a substitute for proper pay. We don't have a wage scale. Everyone's salary is reviewed on the day they join the company. There is a company guideline but each boss has the freedom to pay superstars more than plodders.

Everyone in our branches has the opportunity to increase pay substantially through the weekly bonus scheme. It is a simple system that operates the same way in every shop. Each week the total branch wage cost is multiplied by 4.5 (our so-called magic number) to set the weekly target. We pay a 15 per cent bonus on all turnover over the target with no upper limit. The bonus pot is shared between everyone in the branch, according to the hours they worked and their experience. The present branch bonus scheme has been running for 25 years with hardly any adjustment. I dare not change it – I would be lynched.

It creates the adrenaline that runs through the business. As a result, our people are keen to improve their performance. I want them to earn as much money as possible – the bigger their bonus, the bigger our profits. Our job is to help them earn more money and we do that by providing loads of training.

For many people, bonus earnings are a substantial proportion of their total pay. This has its dangers. Bonuses can go down as well as up, so banks and building societies look at basic pay when lending money or offering a mortgage. To provide stability, we guarantee 90 per cent of last year's total earnings so that nobody suffers unduly from a major drop in business.

Our branch bonus is closely linked to personal performance. This is more difficult to achieve for people at Timpson House, where the bonus is based on company profit. I don't like contrived point-scoring schemes based on personal appraisals; subjective judgment is no substitute for performance measured against a financial target. But there is no reason why exceptional performance can't be rewarded, with a special bonus always sent in a hand-written letter to the employee's home.

I would make two warnings about pay. Even if the company has a financial crisis, never have a wage freeze. There is no point in penalising the people you will rely on most to get you out of the difficulty. Always check how your pay compares to the rest of the market and make sure you are generous compared to the competition. But whatever you pay, you will never stop some employees being tempted by an offer they can't refuse. Let them go, wish them well and wait. Life with another company may not be as good as they thought. Before long they may ask to come back.

You should also care for your employees' well-being by offering kindness above expectation. From time to time, star performers will slide down the performance league. There is always an explanation. It is usually nothing to do with the business but something in the rest of their lives that has put them off their stride. Many managers would rant and rave about improving performance; you should search for the real reason.

With the trust of your workforce, you will probably be the first person that employees turn to in times of trouble. Within the Timpson community, it is our job to care for and help employees through their difficulties. Many problems are financial. We have a hardship fund to help (currently we have around £200,000 on loan to employees). The causes are nothing exceptional – dental care, house move, rent arrears, car maintenance, dealing with bailiffs. I would much rather solve these problems by lending money, as it reduces the temptation to take it from the till.

Other problems are not financial. Colleagues have free access to an independent helpline that provides financial advice but also deals with bereavement, divorce, drugs and alcohol. Our helpline puts them in touch with an expert but often they prefer to speak to their boss, as someone they know and trust. We have devised a special training course to help with counselling but we don't train managers to be experts. Rather, we teach them how to listen and put employees in touch with the people who can give them the help that they really need.

Timpson employees get a lot of other benefits. To celebrate our centenary in 2003, we gave everyone their birthday off. This benefit is so popular it is now a permanent feature. Significant birthdays – 18, 21, 30, 40, 50, 60 – are celebrated with a bottle of champagne. Everyone who gets married receives a special £100, plus an extra week off. Our maternity and paternity leave goes beyond the statutory requirements. Expectant mothers receive Mothercare vouchers and a special surprise to celebrate the birth.

For me, Christmas parties are a chore. I don't want to be cast as Scrooge, so we fund the festivities. I don't turn up. Years ago, I grew wary of being dragged on the dance floor by an employee keen to win a bet, or being prodded by a pickled employee who wanted to tell me how to run the business.

Parties at other times of the year are more important. They are optional perks for which the company gets more credit. I still don't turn up, believing most employees would rather get lathered at the company's expense without having me around as a witness. (I do turn up at the New Year's Eve party at our pub, the White Eagle. It's the only time in the year that I go behind the bar in order to escape the kisses from party-goers at midnight.)

I believe in parties, where employees can enjoy themselves at our expense. But I won't pay 100 per cent. It works much better if every participant pays a percentage, except on special occasions when we celebrate success.

We have regular award ceremonies – usually held in a marquee in our garden – but they are never annual events. Once an event happens every year, it is taken for granted.

It is easy to find a reason to celebrate success. We presented our Millennium Awards in 2000 and our Centenary Awards in 2003. (When we refitted shops with a new design scheme in 1995, we put "established 1903" on our fascias. The date was a bit of a guess but it demonstrated our experience. It gave us an excuse to celebrate 100 years of shoe repairing eight years later.)

We take award-giving very seriously. Candidates are nominated by their colleagues, with the top three invited to the event with their partners and the winner's name revealed by opening an envelope. With so many star employees at Timpson you have to be pretty good to win. We want the winners to enjoy their success – it often leads to publicity in their local press – it's all part of being a great place to work.

Bill Platt has a special job. He is our People Person, responsible for championing the interests of employees. He visits people in hospital, buys everyone an ice cream when the office is sweltering, organises our holiday homes and DVD lending library. He compiles our "Who's Who" (a pictorial directory of every employee) and he organises days out – trips on the canal, to the races and shopping trips abroad.

This is part of a big nationwide social programme that includes golf and football tournaments, paint-balling, clay pigeon shooting and plenty of nights outs.

At Timpson House, we have installed a gym and have regular visits from a masseur. We are about to build a tennis court. We have three season tickets so that colleagues can watch my team, Manchester City. To give supporters in other parts of the country a chance to see their team, we now also have tickets for Celtic, Rangers, Portsmouth, Newcastle United and Fulham. We have debenture tickets for Wembley that are not just for the directors. Everyone can apply to see sporting events and concerts at a fraction of the full cost.

You don't have to build a palace to create a great place to work – it's people that make a happy workplace, not buildings or design consultants – but good design can make a difference, especially if it enhances the company culture.

James and I were amazed by an office we visited in Helsinki – the headquarters of Sol, a cleaning company with attitude. The converted film studio had graffiti on the walls and comic statues of the owners sitting on a bench, watching employees. They symbolised the unconventional approach that the chairman, Liisa Joronen, had used to create success. There was no paper, no telephone system, no personal desk space, but total freedom to work where and when you wanted. The work space should be an expression of company character. It should also be set up to satisfy the needs of employees – not the chairman's wife!

We have four holiday homes in Blackpool, Bournemouth, Spain and Turkey. Currently we are renovating a cottage in Snowdonia that will become holiday home number five. Accommodation is free. Anyone who has been with the company for over a year can apply. Not surprisingly, we are oversubscribed.

My favourite benefits are those that come with a big surprise, such as Brian Elliott's retirement gift. Brian had been an area manager for many years and was one of our first regional managers. He had played a big part in the development of our company in the 1980s and 1990s. His fellow regional managers invited him to a meeting at Luton Airport, saying they had booked a conference room. Brian turned up in his suit with a briefcase. He was unaware that his wife had packed his holiday clothes and given them to his colleagues. There was no meeting – they were booked on a flight to Spain for a three-night retirement party.

I first met Brian Armstrong 35 years ago, when he was manning a little workshop in the back of our shoe shop in Accrington. Brian is a great John Wayne fan. On John Wayne's birthday, he decorates his branch with posters of the film star. James and I asked Brian and his wife to come to my office for tea, in order to mark his 40 years with the business. Brian was halfway through his cake when we revealed our secret. We handed him an envelope with tickets for a week's holiday in Iowa, John Wayne's birthplace. They had a wonderful time. Brian was treated like a celebrity and featured in the local press. He was in the papers again when he got home. In fact, stories of Brian's trip created such an interest in Accrington that it increased the number of customers coming into our shop – a surprising return on our investment.

On a visit to Hounslow, I was chatting to our ADM, a good guy who had made a real difference to our business. "I would just like to say thanks," he said, "for allowing me to book the holiday home in Spain for two weeks next year. I know that you don't normally let us book that far ahead but James knows it will be my honeymoon. It has made a big difference to the cost of our wedding."

Thanks like that make us keen to do even more. We are looking at better ways to celebrate a birthday. Instead of just sending a card, how about giving an appropriate personal gift that really shows we care – a round of golf, tickets for concerts or appropriate vouchers – and that makes superstars feel special. These are things that make people go "wow!"

We have launched a new scheme called "Dreams Come True". Since 1987, when we sold the shoe shops and moved to Timpson House, the success of the company has been beyond my wildest dreams. To celebrate, I have asked everyone to tell me their personal dream scenario. And in each month for the next year I will make somebody's dream come true.

We recognise long service. I send a letter and a cheque to mark five, ten, 15, 20, 30, 35 and 40 years. The 25- and 45-year anniversaries are special. Alex and I make these presentations at a lunch party at our house. Out of the workforce of 1,800, we currently have 92 people who have been with the company more than 25 years. Every year about ten more join that elite club.

The long service lunch provides me with an annual reminder that looking after people is so worthwhile.

Over the past few years we have introduced lots of new things designed to make Timpson a better place to work. When we started giving employees their birthdays off, an accountant asked me how much it cost. I thought this an irrelevant question but, to some, a wide-ranging employee care programme is an enormous expense. In my view, it's a cost that should never be cut. Even if the business is going through a bad time we should treat employees as well as we possibly can. If we do that, they in turn will be great at looking after our customers.

LESSONS

**Looking after star employees is a top priority.
Here are just some ways to create a great place to work.**

- **Meet as many people as possible as often as you can**
- **And listen to them!**
- **Have attractive pay**
  Pay your superstars
  at higher rates
  Have a good bonus scheme
  Have a minimum earnings
  guarantee
  Aim to increase pay
  for everyone
- **Give regular, tangible praise**
  Chocolates, wine, a day off,
  a night out, mention people
  in your newsletter, hand-write
  letters, personal gifts, a cheque
  (with the tax paid), chairman's
  special award

- **Ensure their personal welfare**
  Hardship fund
  Independent helpline
  Create a caring culture
- **Have loads of extra benefits**
  Birthday off, football tickets,
  free ice cream, gym and
  masseur, wedding present and
  extra week off, extra maternity/
  paternity leave and Mothercare
  vouchers, special birthday
  champagne, golf tournament,
  "Dreams Come True", Football
  Championship
- **Celebrate success**
  Long service lunch
  Office barbeque
  Award dinner
  Long service awards

Chapter 9

CUSTOMERS COME SECOND

"We develop our business by looking after customers, not by sticking to some rule laid down by Head Office" Barbara Mead

Being great at looking after customers is the vital ingredient of retail success. It's so obvious. You don't need market research and focus groups to tell you that looking after customers is good for business – it is common sense.

Our business repairs shoes, cuts keys, repairs watches and does engraving. We have to do all these jobs well but, if we want customers to come back, we must be nice to them. We spend less than £20,000 annually on advertising – most of that went on sponsoring Manchester City's scoreboard. Other businesses spend millions and then put customers off with poor, even pathetic, service.

Why don't these companies get it? Perhaps the chief executive is stuck in an office, never seeing the world through the eyes of his customers.

It is amazing how many companies take customers for granted and provide shoddy service. Petrol retailers spend lots of money putting ten pumps on the forecourt and three tills behind the counter – but you still have to queue. Why? Because there is seldom more than one till in operation. To save wages, they only have two staff members per shift. One works the till while the other fills shelves, makes the tea and chats to the person serving customers. Petrol retailers can't see their bad service from a desk at head office. The quality of customer care is not revealed on a separate line in their management accounts but it has a major influence on profit.

In the 1980s B&Q was so paranoid about shoplifting and stock losses that staff were mainly employed to stop customers pinching their products. Sales assistants did not assist customers; they made them stick to the rules. When B&Q increased staff levels and employed nice people to help their customers, sales rose dramatically.

Self-service, which started in the 1960s, stopped sales staff talking to customers. Their new job was to fill shelves, complete forms and operate the computer-driven till. Recently, supermarkets have started to worry about customer care once more. They now expect staff to answer customer queries and walk with them to the products they want to buy.

Ryanair and EasyJet make a point of being pernickety, inflexible and blunt with customers. They are the exception that proves my rule. They have successfully linked minimal service with cheap prices. Don't expect sympathy if you check in late. Few businesses can rely purely on price; I wonder which of these airlines will be the first to show a more compassionate attitude to customers.

Every day we see signs of lousy service. It is not necessary for customers to queue more than ten minutes to buy a magazine at WHSmith at Manchester Airport. Hospitals should not make appointments that they know will involve a one-hour wait. Banks should not charge £20 for a 60p overdraft.

It is amazing that business executives forget that there is a customer's point of view. After all, they are shoppers themselves. Every retail experience should sharpen their awareness of how their own customers are thinking. Instead, as soon as they walk through the office door, many remove their consumer hat. That's especially if they run a call centre.

Call centres are the shining beacon of poor customer care, particularly if you ring to complain. My worst experiences have been with BT. (Thankfully, they are now showing signs of improvement.) My phone calls led to several letters of complaint. BT responded with comments such as: "Thank you for going to the trouble to write" and "Your feedback is invaluable in our quest to provide a better service" and "We currently fall short of the standard of service we would normally wish to provide but I assure you our current major investment programme [called something like System 08, Super Plug or Sat Box] is designed to drive our dedication to deliver a totally focused service early in the next decade".

Some shops are full of rules. They have posters telling customers what they can't do: "We don't accept £50 pound notes", or "no change for the car park" and "only two school children in the shop at once". I keep meeting sales assistants who tell me why something can't be done, with lines such as "I'm not allowed to…" or "Ii's company policy to…" or "you will have to speak to the manager".

With so many rules, you can get a reputation for good service just by never saying "no". "You can use our loo", "you can use our phone", "we will give you directions to the Post Office", " we will change a £50 pound note", " we will give you change for the car park" and "you can use your credit card to buy a key ring for 25p". These things may not make sense to the finance department but will be appreciated by customers. And they will come back and spend more money.

Since we opened our pub, I have taken special note of other publicans. A free house, close to a cricket ground that relies on the players and spectators for much of their weekend trade, had a big notice in their garden that banned customers from moving their chairs to watch the cricket. Another local pub with a garden was so worried that customers would run off without paying that they erected an 8ft by 6ft sign, showing its list of regulations for customers eating outside. Most of these rules are misguided attempts to police unwelcome and dishonest clients at the expense of the majority who are squeaky clean. Trust people and they will become loyal customers.

Customers get abandoned by management in the cause of cost-cutting and central control. When we bought Sketchley, we discovered dry cleaning attracts a lot of complaints. The Sketchley complaints department had been made "more efficient" by the introduction of voice mail; this saved £35,000 a year and turned mild complaints into totally dissatisfied customers.

Good customer care builds reputations. Pret a Manger makes sure that you don't wait, by having loads of staff behind the counter calling "next, please". Carphone Warehouse and Majestic Wine have staff who really know their products and give valuable service. Every AA man who has come to my rescue has turned up quickly, solved my problem and been really nice about it. John Lewis might be a bit stuffy but they are consistently civil and professional.

These successes don't come easy. Pret a Manger test-shop its service in every branch every week. Carphone Warehouse and Majestic Wine look for recruits with A-levels and degrees. John Lewis has built its reputation since John Spedan Lewis gave ownership to his employees in 1929.

The level of service in any business is determined by the passion of the person at the top. A company that receives 450 complaints in a year usually points to the two million customers that it serves, believing that the majority is satisfied. The consumer champion looks into the detail of these complaints and uses them to improve its service to customers.

To the enlightened, the real question is: how can we look after customers even better? I have read some of the hundreds of books that have been written about customer service. All have examples of employees who have gone the extra mile to look after their customers. We have our own customer heroes who are just as good as those that work for Starbucks, South West Airlines, Nordstrom and Richer Sounds.

I see wonderful examples of customer care on my travels. PJ (O'Sullivan) in Reading and Bob Northover in Taunton have a similar approach to retailing. As soon as the shop opens they are on stage. They entertain their customers and take as much money as possible. Both have been in their shops so long that it is not "a Timpson" – it is their shop. Customers have become their friends; they know most of their names. In Bob's shop, I witnessed a remarkable example of customer service – and it wasn't Bob behind the counter. One of his team served a senior citizen who had a scooter with a special basket to carry her dog. She wanted a bikers' jacket for the pet. Amazingly, Bob's team agreed. I watched while the dog stood on the counter to be measured for his new leather jacket.

Good staff, unsure whether the key they have cut will work, will tell customers not to pay there and then. They say: "When you get home, check it works and settle up when you are next in town." Adrian in Beverley went one better. His customer wanted a full sole and heel that would take 30 minutes. "I'm going to have to leave it," said his customer. "Just do the heels, as my bus leaves in 20 minutes." "Where do you live?" asked Adrian. "I'll drive you home."

When I was last in Hammersmith, John Whelan was talking to a customer who had brought in six pairs of shoes. At the same time, he was repairing someone else's stilettos and telling his colleagues where to find a watch that was ready for another customer. John would be amazed that I was amazed. That is the way he runs his shop every day.

Improving customer care is a job for life. In 1997, I discovered *The Nordstrom Way*, a book about the American chain of department stores. Nordstrom has an odd company structure: customers are at the top and the chairman is at the bottom. Their sales assistants have the most important jobs. Everyone else is there to give them help and support.

It all seemed to fit. I realised that the best way to help our staff give great service in Peterhead, Brighton, Plymouth and Llanelli was to trust them to do it their way. I thought of our shops that gave exceptional service and realised they were all run by managers with a bubbly personality. Given freedom they will provide their own individual style of personal service.

You can't create good customer service by imposing a set of rules or rigid training guidelines. You won't get people to give great service by issuing a code of service. You need to pick great people and let them display their personality. The saying "the customer comes first" is misleading. Customers do not come first. Our top priority is to look after the people who serve them.

I had discovered the two secrets behind great customer care. Secret one is to trust the people who serve your customers to do it their way. Secret two is to pick the right people.

We are not asking for much. We just want people who are good at engraving, repairing shoes, cutting keys, repairing watches, looking after merchandise, filling in figures, love serving customers, have a great personality and put the money in the till. Surprisingly, we have found lots of people who can do all that and more.

With people like this, we don't need rules but we do need regular customer care training. This must never stop. Everyone should attend a new customer care course every three years and each course should be better than the last one. It's an odd sort of training course, because we don't tell people what to do – remember this is upside-down management. You can learn more about customer care while waiting in a queue at Tesco than through formal training. That's why our courses start with a bit of shopping. We send participants down the high street with a shopping list; they report back on their good and bad experiences as a customer.

The detailed content of our training courses is not particularly important; it is the discussion that really matters. We want people to spend time thinking and talking about service, suggesting ideas to each other. We don't tell them what to do. We don't even tell people to smile. We want them to get the customer to smile – that is the sign of really good customer care.

Customer care has now become a crusade headed by Mike Donoghue, who became our customer care controller in 2005. He and his team deal with some of our most difficult customers, but he doesn't just run a customer complaint department. He is responsible for promoting the cause of customer care throughout the company. Here are some of the most important elements of our customer care campaign.

POLICY STATEMENT

In every shop we display a notice that says: "The staff in this shop have my total authority to do whatever they can to give you amazing service." It is above the door, facing towards colleagues behind the counter as a constant reminder.

THE BONUS

The way to maximise the bonus is to look after lots of customers. Sluggish service occurs at motorway service stations because it doesn't make any difference to the sales staff whether they take £250 or £1,000. They don't get a bonus. Our scheme puts buzz into our business and customers notice it.

SKILL POINTS

We have a simple customer care checklist that our assessors use during a day in a branch. Many thought colleagues would up their game while being observed and give a false impression. This has not proved to be the case. You can put on an act for 30 minutes but it is difficult to sustain the performance all day. Customer care skill points now rank alongside craft skills for bonus purposes. There is a difference: customer care skills are re-tested every two years.

MYSTERY SHOPPING

Since 1996, we have seen our branches through the eyes of a customer by reading reports from mystery shoppers. But we recently abandoned mystery shopping in favour of mystery DVDs. Instead of providing a written report, our mystery shoppers now act as a human tripod with a small hidden camera and then send us the DVD. I got the idea from a lady at Kurt Geiger who I met at a conference. She told me that mystery videos had made a big difference to her business. I tried them with some trepidation, wondering what our people would think. I was in for a shock. They welcomed the move and appreciated the truth. Seeing themselves serving customers taught them how to improve their service skills.

CUSTOMER REPLY CARDS

I first used customer reply cards in 1976. I copied one that I found in Chicago. It had the snappy phrase "Help Us to Help You". I have always been amazed at the level of response and the significant number of customers who go to the trouble of adding detailed comments. Well over 90 per cent give glowing compliments. This is reassuring, not just to me but also to the people who work in our shops. They appreciate seeing what customers have to say. A customer compliment is a superb form of praise and gives colleagues increased pride in their job.

We now take customer comments even more seriously. We have a scoring system that we discovered in a book called *The Ultimate Question*. The question we ask is: "On a scale of one to ten, how keen would you be to recommend us to a friend or colleague?" The calculation is simple. We add the cards with nine or ten and divide by all responses with one to six. That produces our customer loyalty ratio – and that measures the quality of our customer care.

SHOP DISPLAYS

Every retail shop displays merchandise and advertises its services. Very few promote customer care. Adrian Jennison in Beverley has turned part of his branch into a shop notice board, containing press cuttings, customer compliments, skill certificates and pictures of the staff's latest night out. It is not what you expect to find in a multiple business but that is the point; it shows service is personal.

NO EPOS

Plenty of shops keep you waiting while they put purchases through the till, so that they can keep the computerised stock control up to date. I faced a problem when waiting at a supermarket checkout because I was guilty of picking up a jar of gherkins that didn't have a bar code. Before I could say "36p", the check-out girl rang her bell. She waved my gherkins in the air. A young man took the gherkins on a gentle stroll across the store. He returned with the news that they were, indeed, 36p. If they had believed me we would all have saved five minutes and a lot of bother.

My gherkins were trouble-free compared with Kerry's swedes. When he was our training supervisor, Kerry was shopping at his local Sainsbury's. He spotted a special offer "Free swedes if you buy 5lbs of potatoes". Kerry already had plenty of potatoes but is passionate about swedes. He took a packet of swedes to the checkout.

"Where are the potatoes?" asked the assistant.

"I don't want potatoes. I just want Swedes," replied Kerry.

"But you can't have them without the potatoes," said the assistant.

"I'll pay for the swedes," said Kerry.

"You can't pay for them. They are free," said the assistant.

"Well I don't want them for nothing," said an exasperated Kerry. "Tell me how much they are and I'll pay for them."

"Sorry, I can't do that."

(Eventually Kerry found a supervisor who allowed him to buy the swedes for the price of a pack of potatoes.)

Fortunately, we run quite happily without EPOS. As a result, customers get quicker service.

HIDDEN EXTRAS

I love it when our branch colleagues use their initiative to do things that would be against most company rules. Some shops have newspapers for customers to read. Others provide sweets for children. Some even make customers a cup of tea. They are happy to look after customers' shopping. They let them use our loo. Most shopkeepers find an excuse to avoid this sort of free service, often blaming health and safety. We encourage colleagues to ignore imaginary red tape. They amaze customers by doing helpful things, such as carrying shopping to their customer's car.

CHILDLINE

Customers like the way we charge for small jobs. Bits of stitching or holes in a belt are done for charity; we ask customers to put £1 in the box for Child Line. It creates more customer compliments than anything else we do.

CUSTOMER CARE AWARDS

In 2007, we held our first customer care award lunch in a marquee at my home in Cheshire. Our superstars came from all over the country to collect their awards. Here are some of the stories that made them winners.

Arnaud Gois, in Villiers Street in London, had a customer who had just broken up from her partner. She poured out her troubles to Arnaud.

When she returned to collect her shoes, Arnaud, using all his native French charm, had bought her a bunch of flowers.

Hayley McGinley had just opened our new shop in Penrith, which offers a dry cleaning service. The local contractor, who was doing the dry cleaning, lost a customer's suit. Hayley sorted out the problem and the garment was delivered to the customer's home in time for the holiday. When the customer went to see Hayley on her next visit to Penrith, Hayley had a bunch of flowers waiting to help her say sorry.

Ashley from Pontypridd saved a bemused best man from extreme embarrassment when he corrected a competitor's unfortunate spelling mistake on the bridesmaids' engraved gifts.

"How much do I owe?" asked the best man.

"Nothing," replied Ashley.

"It was my mistake," the customer insisted.

"Don't worry," said Ashley, "call it a wedding present."

KEEP CAMPAIGNING

If you don't keep talking about customer care, standards will slip. We need to keep finding new ways to spread an old message. Things improve when we hold a customer care week or put a sandwich board outside the shops that claims we offer the best service in Britain.

I haven't mentioned complaints. Most complaints are justified.

They are a great opportunity, not a nuisance. Most of the complimentary letters that we receive are about how we dealt with a complaint. It is the perfect opportunity to amaze customers. Ninety-eight per cent of the keys we cut work properly; the two per cent that don't work give us real opportunities to impress customers. Complaints tell you how you can make the business better. Complaints are nothing to be ashamed about.

Get a complaining customer on your side by admitting the mistake. Take personal responsibility, even if you didn't do the job yourself. If the mistake was done by a competitor, still provide compensation. It's a cheap way to win a new customer.

Find ways to give customers more than they ever expected. If a key doesn't work, cut two free ones and give money to compensate for the customer's journey back into town. Some colleagues are reluctant to give my money away. I say, "please be generous". Complaints cost us less than £15,000 a week. Spent wisely, it is very cheap advertising.

Many companies design their complaints policy with a nightmare customer in mind. We take a different view. Our colleagues can spend up to £500 to deal with a complaining customer, but they don't have to give in to a bully.

We often get Mr Nasty on the phone to our customer care department at Timpson House where Mike, Joan and Mandy display the most amazing patience and expertise. Often Mr Nasty doesn't want compensation – he just likes complaining. We don't want Mr Nasty. I would be happy if he never shopped with us again. But he is an odd sort of bloke and the chances are you will see him again next week.

Complaints show that our customers care enough about our business to let us know where we are going wrong. This constant feedback is just what we need because the campaign for better service will never end. They are helping us improve the most important part of our business.

LESSONS

- Make customer care a fundamental part of the culture
- Give your staff freedom and trust them to give great service
- Avoid rules – for both staff and customers
- Customer care training never stops
- Praise the customer care champions – pass on compliments and present your own service awards to superstars
- However good you think you are, always keep looking for ways to improve customer care

THE TWO SECRETS:

1 Trust the people who serve your customers with the freedom to do it their way

2 Pick the right people

Chapter 10

UPSIDE-DOWN MANAGEMENT

"It's not for wimps. It's for managers who have the courage to show what they are made of" Simon Childs

Years ago, we were like any other business. We had our rules, called standing orders for shoe repair factories (SOSRF). Our area managers acted like dictators. They inspected shops with a clipboard and disciplined those people who didn't toe the line. Head office ran the business by issuing orders. Everyone was controlled by the annual budget.

What a contrast with today. Our upside-down management chart shows colleagues at the top and directors at the bottom.

The heroes are our area managers. Their role is critical. Without their support, our new style management was doomed to failure. When upside-down management was launched, there were 14 areas. Each manager covered about 25 shops, with the help of three area assistants. These area assistants were unhappy. Having been promoted to the area team, they were treated like little boys. Their area managers sent them on errands rather than giving them real responsibility. They acted like relief shop managers, spending their time covering staff shortages, illness and holidays.

One week, when I visited some shops with an area manager, I soon realised there was a long way to go before upside-down management would work properly.

"The problem is," he said, "I can't find the time to recruit. I spend my day dealing with everyday problems and with staff who are below standard."

"Why do you keep them if they are no good?" I asked.

"Because I am short of staff," he replied.

"But," I said, "if you let your assistants help run the area instead of running shops, you would have the time you need for recruitment."

"That may be so," he said, "but I wouldn't trust some of them to do the important jobs. At the end of the day, you hold me responsible."

At the end of the conversation he revealed to me the real problem.

"Apart from anything else," he said, "if I let my assistants do my job, what will be left for me to do?"

It was my fault; I should have anticipated the problem. When I started to talk about upside-down management, I just thought about shops and the colleagues serving customers. It had not occurred to me upside-down management would also apply to the rest of the business. I had changed my management style. I had changed the role of area managers. I hadn't taught them how to do their new job.

I wrote a guide for area managers that explained the new role in words and pictures. It described area managers as leaders who set an example, helping their assistants run the area on their behalf. It showed how to be a delegator and communicator and how to represent the interests of their people to head office. It illustrated the importance of building a team, dealing with problems, and being an agony aunt. I told them to spend time thinking about strategy, giving priority to having the right people in the right place.

The manual made it clear that upside-down management gave area managers freedom in the same way as everyone else. They could do their job in the way they thought best, with only four rules:

1. Have at least the minimum number of staff to cover the shops.
2. Give great customer care.
3. Have good housekeeping.
4. Keep everything legal.

They could achieve these objectives in any way they wanted.

My guide filled 250 pages but I did not send it out. I went through it, page by page, at a series of conferences. Three times a year, I revealed a little bit more of the area managers' job and then got them to discuss it in detail. Gradually, the message started to sink in. Two area managers completely changed their routine, delegating day-to-day management to their assistants and using the extra time to recruit necessary new staff. Their success set an example. Upside-down management started to become part of the Timpson culture.

It took three years before we made real progress. It would not have worked without the benefit of a good bonus scheme. For positive people, the new-found freedom provided an opportunity to use their initiative and increase their bonus.

Upside-down management doesn't suit everyone. Those who like to stick to rules and lazy people, who expect to get money for nothing, are untouched by it. For most people, shop work provides a humdrum 9-to-5 existence stocking shelves, updating the till and looking forward to the time to go home.

For people with character, upside-down management gives the chance to make the shop their own. It might say "Timpson" above the door, but we want our customers to feel the shop belongs to the person who manages it. We want managers to run their own fun days, organise charity promotions and invent new displays.

Upside-down management started with our shops. It wasn't long before we changed the outlook from head office. Now we have stopped talking about head office. It is Timpson House, there to help branch colleagues make more money. I expected this conversion to be the most difficult task but it wasn't. Timpson House quickly changed from a dictatorial centre of control to a company-wide helpline. To emphasise the helpline role, we ran a series of syndicate groups for everyone who works at Wythenshawe. The meetings started with a presentation, describing the history of customer care at Timpson. Then the groups were asked to discuss five questions:

- Who are your customers?
- What do they expect?
- How do you amaze them?
- What do you need to improve the service you give?
- What is stopping us putting that improvement into practise?

They all agreed: their job was to look after the people who work in the field, serving our customers.

Upside-down management is not a quick fix. You must be patient. Getting it going is like seeding a new lawn. First a tiny bit appears, then another; it is a long time before the whole lawn is green. It might take time but things continue to get better and better.

We realised how much we had changed after we bought Mr Minit. Our upside-down management style could not have been more different. Minit's head office team controlled everything, relying on EPOS information and seldom visiting the branches.

We found it fairly easy to turn round the Minit shoe repair business. With delegation already ingrained into the Timpson culture, we left it to our area managers who we trusted to get on with the job. They knew how to run shops better than anyone at Timpson House, so it seemed sensible to let them introduce the Timpson name and methods to Minit as soon as possible. Within 18 months they had turned losses into profits of more than £3m.

Upside-down management can't be taken for granted. Other businesses use a more traditional management style; we are the odd ones out. There is this constant, strong magnetic force trying to bring us back in line with the world of command and control. We must keep reminding ourselves why delegation has been so successful. It has been a much better way to run a business, both for the boss and the members of his team. Colleagues enjoy being trusted with the freedom to show their initiative. They don't have to ask for permission to improve the business. The boss avoids micro-management, without having to bother about detail and write lots of rules. The boss can stand back and get a balanced view; time is created to think about strategy.

We have proved it works but it will always be difficult to persuade traditional managers to abandon control and to delegate. They raise two main objections. The first is: "If you are judging me by performance, I must keep control." And the second is: "What will happen to my job if I let others make the day-to-day decisions?"

Upside-down management only works with the right personalities. We want leaders who feel privileged to be the boss, realising they are the caretakers of our company culture. Ambition shouldn't be purely personal. We don't want selfish, career-minded big shots who are only in it for themselves. Some companies may see these types as high achievers but they don't fit in at Timpson. We don't want executives who are using our business as a stepping stone in their career. We want characters that are committed to our company. Being a boss in upside-down management is an unselfish role that is a million miles away from *The Apprentice*. This is not an aggressive hire-and-fire business. It is a family, where people work together like friends and have the courage to stand back while team members learn by making mistakes.

But a boss in an upside-down management world can't opt out. Delegation creates more time but there is still plenty for the boss to do. The boss can't delegate strategy. It is his job to pick the right people and, although you give your team freedom to run the day-to-day business, you must continue to watch them carefully. You watch by getting round the business and listening. You talk to everyone at every level and join in anyone else's meeting. Our culture encourages you to cut across the management structure because there are few politics. There is a notice at the entrance to Timpson House: "Everyone is requested to leave politics in the car park."

No boss knows everything. The more help he can get from his team, the better. But the team needs to know what is going on. In upside-down management there are no secrets. Everyone is told everything, including our profit and cash flow. Facts are only confidential for personal or legal reasons. Instead of issuing orders, our bosses give guidelines, hand out praise, celebrate success and help solve personal problems.

In the old days, a shop visit was an inspection, running fingers along the pelmet to look for dust. We still have inspections but, today, the main reason is to keep in touch with reality.

Area managers must think in terms of 30 shops instead of one. Some situations are unique to a branch (such as personal problems or road works) but most occur everywhere. A good manager relates what he sees in one shop to the rest of his area. If a good idea works in one place, it will almost certainly work everywhere. The same applies to problems. If one branch gets it wrong, others are probably making the same mistake. If putting coloured keys on a display board has increased sales in one shop, spread it to the rest of the area. If you find the shop is still displaying Christmas posters halfway through January, assume others have made the same mistake and mention it in your weekly newsletter.

In upside-down management, the boss is far from redundant. The boss is a role model. The boss is the team's spokesman, fighting on their behalf. The boss spots the drongos. The boss clamps down on any hint that head office is trying to run the business.

As it develops, more benefits appear. Area manager Darren Brown devised a new role for his mobile managers; instead of restricting responsibility to branch management, he made them full members of his area team. It is working so well that other areas are following his lead. Darren's initiative has changed the future structure of the company. Nine years on, upside-down management feels likepart of our culture, I know it works partly because profits have increased from £2.5m to £12.5m but mainly because our people keep telling me it's a better way to run a business.

LESSONS

How to be an upside-down manager:

- Mastermind the strategy
- Pick the right personalities
- Trust them with authority
- Watch them carefully
- Help your people succeed
- Praise star performers

NO ORDERS
NO SECRETS
NO BIG SHOTS

Chapter 11
TRAINING

"In difficult times many companies cut the training budget. I wouldn't want to be around if you try that on Peter Harris"
John Timpson

I have a confession to make. For years I wasn't a great fan of training. I thought it was an administrative jungle that was full of politics. It soaked up people's time with long meetings and without much benefit. Just shows how wrong you can be.

I have totally changed my mind. Training is the key to improving the business – as long as it is training with a purpose. In our business, training must aim to improve the way we look after customers, help colleagues increase the size of their bonus and develop the management team of the future.

Once we stopped recruiting shoe repairers and concentrated on personality, training became a necessity. But I had already experienced my Eureka moment. I discovered training when talking to Mike Donoghue, who was then our shoe repair product manager. We had just bought Automagic. I was wondering how to control the quality of our shoe repairs.

"What guidelines do we give our colleagues?" I asked Mike with the naiveté of a chairman who had never sat in on a training course.

"There is nothing formal," replied Mike. "Nothing is written down. We ask them to produce a good commercial job."

"What's a good commercial job?" I asked.

"Something that looks good but doesn't take a long time to produce," he replied.

"How do they know how to do it?" I persisted.

"It is handed down from one generation to another," said Mike, "or in our case from cobbler to cobbler."

This didn't seem good enough. Shoe repair was the biggest part of our business but quality control was in the hands of the limp phrase "good commercial job".

"Wait there," I said to Mike, "I've got an idea."

I went to the nearest garden centre and bought three gardening books. The illustrated books by Dr DG Hessayon tell the reader everything in very few words and lots of pictures. They start by telling you the purpose of a fork and spade.

"That's what we need, Mike," I said, when I returned to the office. "Simple pictures to set the standards and tell people how to do the job."

A month later it was Easter – and it never stopped raining. There was no chance of playing golf, so I sat at home writing our very first manual. As someone who has never successfully mended a shoe, I might appear to be the worst person in the world to write a shoe repair manual. That didn't prove to be the case. My lack of knowledge was a distinct advantage. Experts assume too much and don't anticipate simple questions. Things that are blindingly obvious to experts are puzzling to the uninitiated.

The manual worked. It showed how finished repairs should look. It gave a guide on how to get there. I checked it out with a few craftsmen cobblers and they gave their seal of approval.

I then sent myself on a training course. For the first time, I learned how to cut a key, eagerly writing notes for my next manual. To make sure I hadn't missed anything, I sat through the course again. Our key cutting guide is still used today in its original form.

These manuals became an obsession. It was time to teach someone else how to write them. I contacted John Tucker, an ADM from South Wales who had recently been promoted from his branch management in Merthyr Tydfil. We met at a hotel near Walsall and John immediately took on the challenge. He completed our engraving manual a few weeks before he sadly suffered a fatal heart attack. His memory lives on in the shape of our engraving guide.

Fortunately I found other people who could write in pictures rather than words. Helene Shepherd, an area manager, wrote our managers' guide while on maternity leave. ADM Brent Sabey tackled the watch repair guide.

Our recruitment policy brought newcomers with bubbly personalities but no experience. We needed to reinvent the word "apprentice". The basic parts of all our skill guides were put together in an apprentice manual. We persuaded a number of experienced branch managers to become apprentice trainers. We decided the only way to train was to do it in a shop facing real customers. (Mr Minit took a different view. They created a training centre at Sheffield where everyone went on a three-week course. Some people found the experience valuable but the overall results were patchy.)

We started to find that apprentices were producing a better job than some long-service employees, so we extended skill training to everyone. We set skill levels and established rigorous tests. In the beginning, it was difficult to persuade our experts to take a test. We needed an incentive. The initial suggestion was to give £50 for each skill obtained – but we found a better idea when we linked skills to our bonus scheme.

When skill testing started in earnest, we were in for a shock. Some of the old craftsmen were not as good as they thought they were; raw recruits were quicker to learn, especially when it came to computer engraving. I was surprised how readily nearly every one accepted the idea of being tested.

Initially, each skill added an extra percentage to the recipient's bonus. The scheme became even more serious when we changed to a points basis, with every skill point increasing their share of the bonus pot. I knew training had really got into our culture when it cropped up in our everyday language – "How are you doing with your levels?" and "I've only got to answer one more question before I get my level 2". Suddenly things were serious. People took a pride in their performance and everyone put their certificate on the shop wall.

We also introduced off-site courses, starting with a locksmith's course in the early 1990s. Off-site training was essential when we started watch repairs. At first, we relied on experts from outside Timpson but it would have taken too long for a small group to get the message across to 320 branches. James found the answer when he discovered the Horological Centre near Newark, a central resource for the watch repair trade. Within five months we had given everybody the basic knowledge of watch repairs. Some became experts and they helped us take watch repair training in-house, write the manual and produce our first watch repair skill test.

Our most important off-site training course is customer care, which has been a fixed part of our programme for more than ten years. Unlike shoe repairs and key cutting, where once you have got your skills you can claim the t-shirt, you never stop learning about customer care. Every one attends a customer care course every two years.

Shoe repairing at Timpson has come a long way since we produced "a good commercial job". While this was happening, though, we ignored management training until we started upside-down management and realised we had a problem. Upside-down management created a real need for training and my area manager's guide was the first step on the way to our management training scheme.

My love of manuals has continued but I now focus on management.

With the encouragement of James and the assistance of graphic artist Robert Barrow, I produced our first "Mr Men" book, *How to be a Great Boss*, which explains upside-down management in as few words as possible. More books have followed: *How to be a Great Employee, How to Create a Great Place to Work, How to Create More Time, How to Increase Your Bonus, How to Create Shopping Fun, How to Find Great People.* The next one will be *How to Create a Great Team.* They are the Timpson management text books.

When the shoe repair business split from the shoe shops in 1987, we lost our training centre. For 15 years, courses were held in hotel conference centres. When we opened our new training centre, we gained a lot by gathering people from round the country at Timpson House. It makes people feel closer to our culture.

Our management training is in its infancy but is already a way of Timpson life, with courses ranging from interviewing skills to time management.

Every year the training budget goes up. Money isn't the problem; the difficulty is time. Area managers often feel that training courses get in the way, but we need to encourage them to release people to attend courses and take advantage of training. Soon there won't be a choice. We are committed to train everybody to develop their talent to its full potential.

Our career booklet, which charts every move from apprentice to regional manager, is more than a manifesto. It is a promise. Career training is recorded in a log book. It is a four-page record of every major management task completed – stocktaking, back-to-work interviews, opening a new shop, health and safety audits. This is one box-ticking exercise that has my blessing. It is a simple reminder that everyone needs to learn by experience.

Some of the best training goes beyond the normal workplace. These are tasks that stretch the imagination and bring people face to face with their own personality. Our management training can include some special challenges such as running someone else's area, chairing a conference or helping run our pub, the White Eagle.

Our area manager meetings have become more like a six-monthly outward bound course. Area managers don't want to sit in a classroom, listening to lectures from department heads. They learn much more by talking to each other in the bar late into the night. These days, most of the conference is held outside. Abseiling, deep sea fishing, raft building, archery, paint balling, orienteering, camping and clay pigeon shooting have all been on our agenda during the past two years.

SOME WORDS OF WARNING

Training doesn't always work. It doesn't work with a dumb pupil. It doesn't work with lousy presenters. It is a waste of time training without a purpose.

Training can't be left to the training department. It is the biggest opportunity to communicate with colleagues. Feel free to gatecrash any training course – you need to know what your people are being told.

I am wary of outside trainers and government training schemes. Few of them understand our business. When I turned our Health and Safety guidelines into few words and lots of pictures, I was told the HSE wouldn't approve as I hadn't followed their guidelines. So our manual now has my illustrated guide in the front and the official bit in the back. Guess which one people read.

We did the same thing for employment law when we produced *How to Avoid an Employment Tribunal*. Civil servants should realise that people don't read words, they look at pictures.

Everyone is involved in training. Many shop managers provide apprentice training while others teach specialist skills such as jewellery repairs. The training department is there to help them do it.

The ultimate responsibility for training lies firmly with the individual. Every person is responsible for their own training because if they don't want to get involved it is a waste of time. In theory, our training courses are optional but people who don't attend are unlikely to make much progress.

I can't see a future without training. We are a service business and must have people who know what they are doing. New recruits bring their personality, we teach them everything else. To flourish, the business will need to keep changing – and you can't create change without training.

I have done a complete about-turn. I was once a real cynic. Today, I am one of training's biggest fans. It is at the centre of the company's future. I never cut the training budget but always keep a close eye on how the money is spent.

LESSONS

- **Training with a purpose**
  Improve customer service
  Increase individual's bonus
- **Use pictures with few words**
- **Appoint good apprentice trainers**
- **Develop respected skill tests**
- **Link skills to the bonus scheme**
- **Make training fun**
- **Develop individual talent to its potential**
- **Everyone has responsibility for their own training**
- **Training is the best way to communicate**
- **Never cut the training budget**
- **Watch how the money is spent**
- **Gatecrash some courses**

Chapter 12
DISCRIMINATE AGAINST DRONGOS

❝You've got to be hungry – some people lack the drive to enjoy the bonus❞
Richard Bujnicki

This is a short chapter with a big message. It is not particularly politically correct but there is no easy way to talk about drongos – our name for those people who make little or no contribution to the business.

We hire for attitude. We look for personalities with a warrior spirit. We look for people who care and know how to have fun. Sometimes we get it wrong. They might fool us at an interview but, before long, they reveal themselves. Here are some warning signs:

■ They turn up late.
■ They throw sickies.
■ They spend time talking to mates on the phone.
■ They read a newspaper behind the counter.
■ They are slow to learn but quick to nip out for a cigarette.
■ Their girlfriend calls for a 20-minute chat.
■ They play the fool at training courses.

They always have someone else to blame. Whatever they do, it is never their fault. The one thing drongos are good at is making excuses: "It wasn't me"; "the traffic was bad"; "me Mam was ill"; "sorry, I'm not in uniform because someone pinched my tie."

There are two top excuses for hanging on to drongos:

1. We are short of staff.
2. Employment law makes it difficult to get rid of them.

Let's deal with the staff shortage cop-out first. You are better off without drongos, however short of staff you are.

One area manager had an impossible drongo apprentice in a potentially high-turnover shop. Sales were well down on last year. The assistant manager left because he couldn't stand working with the drongo any longer. Sales fell further. "There is nothing I can do," said the area manager. "I am so short of staff I just need a pair of hands." A fortnight later, the drongo took a week off. He claimed pneumonia but failed to produce a sick note.

The manager was left on his own. Turnover rose by 40 per cent. He was taking much more money than he achieved with three of them. That's the general rule – every time you say goodbye to a drongo, turnover gets better.

In employment law, government appears to side with the underdog. We want to discriminate against drongos but the law wants to protect them. Don't blame the government. The real culprits are consultants, who produce guidelines designed to keep you out of an employment tribunal. Most HR directors attend breakfast seminars to get up-to-date advice on the safest policy to inoculate your company against any attack from a disenchanted employee. As a result, personnel policy fills three large box files and managers are so frightened that, instead of telling drongos they are useless, they give them extra training.

Our area teams spend five times as long with drongos compared with everyone else. So management time is spent helping people who are no good and have no intention of improving.

We are all playing a silly game. We don't want these people. We don't want jobsworths, moody, idle or careless people, selfish people who have no interest in our business. These are people who haven't even "got it a little bit" – they haven't "got it" at all. The only sensible use of management time is to get rid of them as quickly, as fairly and as neatly as possible.

It is a chore to go through the counselling, oral warning, written warnings and getting the paperwork correct, but most drongos get the message after the first warning letter. The disciplinary route might be standard practice but, to me, it is deceitful. It is a poorly-disguised plot to manage people out of the business. It is much better to be totally honest and tell the drongo immediately that there is no future role and then say sorry with worthwhile compensation. Most appreciate an unofficial chat that isn't recorded in the paperwork. It often avoids the need for all the disciplinary procedure.

Although it isn't following the HR consultant's manual, we encourage this direct approach under a scheme we call "Parting as Friends". We hired the drongo in the first place, so we should say sorry by offering sufficient practical and financial assistance to help him or her move on.

Don't be mean. The full disciplinary procedure can take months. So an eight-week pay-off could be a good investment for you and a welcome windfall for the drongo. To complete the package, offer to help them find a suitable job elsewhere.

Occasionally, you come across a drongo determined to take you to task, but for most it is not in their nature. They are not good at determination.

In ten years, only two drongos have taken us to an employment tribunal. It was worth paying up, just to see the smile on the faces of my superstars who were so relieved to see them go.

Chapter 13
LEADERSHIP

"It is different being part of a private business that takes a long-term view"
Paresh Majithia

Every business needs a leader. Leaders have more influence on the future of a company than anyone – including the leader – ever imagines.

Marks & Spencer was built by Simon Marks and then Lord Sieff. They imposed their personality on the business and made everyone follow their very high standards. Lord Rayner, followed by Richard Greenbury, lacking the same flair, ran M&S by numbers. They were both keen to lead the first retail company to make £1bn profits. They got there at the expense of customer care and store appearance. Their successors, Roger Holmes and Luc Vandevelde, relied on professional management and consultants to help get M&S out of a hole. They both failed. Stuart Rose took charge and brought the company back to the basics of good service, good merchandise and well laid out stores. The consultants and professional managers may have understood the principles but didn't have the personality of Stuart Rose to make it happen.

Iceland, the high street food chain, was started in 1970 when Malcolm Walker opened a shop in Oswestry. By 1975, there were 15 Iceland stores in North Wales and the north-west, supported by a cold store in Rhyl. The business steadily expanded. By 1984, Iceland had 81 stores when it floated; the initial public offer was 113 times oversubscribed. Late in 1988, it won a fiercely contested bid for its much larger, southern-based rival Bejam. The Bejam units were converted to the Iceland format, creating a truly national chain of 465 stores.

By 1995, Iceland could claim 25 years of consistent profit growth. It had 752 stores. But it was facing intensifying competition from the supermarkets. To fight back, Walker led a massive programme of innovation. This included the introduction of national home delivery and the development of a wide range of new products, particularly those promoting healthy eating.

Things went wrong when Iceland bought Booker, the UK's largest cash and carry operator. Walker became non-executive chairman and appointed Stuart Rose (the same guy) to become chief executive of the enlarged group. Shortly after the deal was completed, Stuart Rose left to head Arcadia (which used to be Burton Group), creating a management vacuum. In stepped Bill Grimsey, who had built his reputation at Wickes, the DIY chain.

Within weeks he and his new finance director identified massive problems and launched a major change in direction. Grimsey's declared ambition was to dominate high street food retailing through a renewed focus on core customers and frozen food. Unfortunately, there was a steady decline in customer numbers and turnover while costs escalated. Profits fell and never recovered.

In 2005, the business was bought by a consortium led by Baugur, an Iceland-based investment group. Shareholders received only a fraction of the value that the group had enjoyed at its peak. Baugur split Booker from Iceland, which was placed under the management of Malcolm Walker, who had returned with other executives who had been ejected in 2001.

They found that, in four years, overheads had escalated on a massive scale. Head office employee numbers had grown from 800 to 1,400. Some £16m had been spent on external consultants. The product range had expanded chaotically. Prices were out of line with the market. Morale was at an all-time low. The company was in such a precarious financial state that suppliers couldn't get credit insurance.

Overheads were slashed, the product range reviewed, and prices were cut to restore value to customers. The whole company was reinvigorated. As morale was restored, sales have risen steadily with customers returning to Iceland.

In the financial year to March 2006, like-for-like sales increased by 20 per cent. The company returned a profit and Iceland has a healthy balance sheet once more.

Most books talk about business success. Not enough is written about failure. There are many examples of businesses founded by an entrepreneur with incredible flair, who is then succeeded by a plastic professional manager who loses the plot.

We watched the changes at Johnson the Cleaners. For many years, this was run on conservative lines by Terry Greer and then by Richard Zerny; both had the backing and experience of David Bryant to manage their high street shops. Terry Greer had joined from Sketchley, the 1970s market leader, which had, at one time, tried to take over the Johnson business. While Sketchley floundered under new management following its acquisition of SupaSnaps, Greer and Zerny took advantage of Sketchley's weakness.

When Greer took over, Johnson was trading under several fascias: Smiths the Cleaners, Harris Clean, Pullars of Perth, Zerny's in East Anglia, Hartonclean in the north-east and many others. The Johnson business, based in Merseyside, was the prime mover in the group. When Greer and his team decided to create a nationwide image, Johnson was the natural name to choose. This name change was accompanied by a new branch lay-out that allowed customers to see the dry cleaning in operation.

After Terry Greer retired, Richard Zerny, who had grown up through the family business that bore his name, became managing director. He continued the conservative but sure-footed management style that had been so successful. Johnson wasn't just a high street dry cleaner. It also owned Apparelmaster, providing a workwear service for manufacturing companies from several factories throughout the UK.

Johnson is a publicly quoted company. Its performance, although solid, was not sexy enough for the City. It's probably true that the Johnson style of management was more suited to a private company with a strong family influence. When Zerny retired in 2002, the City wanted to see change. Their sights were set on the short-term; they wanted to lift the share price. In response, the Johnson board selected Stuart Graham to turn the company into a facilities management business, producing services direct to business in preference to its old-fashioned high street presence.

Graham ran up big debts and spent £160m making lots of acquisitions. He failed to increase profits significantly. On the way, the old high street business was losing its charm while the new businesses were losing money. In the end, Graham lost respect and eventually lost his job. He had run Johnson to fulfil a personal ambition that he thought would create a good story for the stock market and drive up the share price. He never had the respect of the core business. During his five years in charge, the Johnson high street chain lacked love. It started to flounder in almost exactly the same way that Sketchley had floundered a decade before.

There are many other examples of leaders who stamped their personalities on a business: George Davies, who built up Next and then almost brought it to bankruptcy; David Jones, who saved Next after George Davies' departure and then revived it; and Charles Dunstone, who has shown everyone else how to run a mobile phone retail chain.

Great leaders are born, not created by a business school. And it can still take years before a great leader is ready for their role. It's no coincidence that so many successful entrepreneurs started work on the shop floor or running a solitary retail outlet. Sir Stanley Kalms, Sir Tom Farmer and Dame Anita Roddick all built their businesses from square one. (I remember when Sir Philip Green was making the tea as a new boy at footwear importer Martin Geminder.)

Many potential leaders fail to take advantage of their inherent talent. They are too lazy or lack the patience needed for long-term success. Great leaders work hard and learn from experience. They are driven personalities with the determination to succeed – winning matters to them. There is a difference between professional managers and self-made men or women. It is bound to be different if you are dealing with your own money, with no hope of a head-hunter helping you move to a bigger job.

Even the most talented future leader needs patience. It takes years to acquire sufficient maturity and experience. Racehorse trainers are careful not to push a potential Grand National winner to jump big fences at a tender age. They are gradually moved from bumper to hurdles and steeple chasing, building up from two miles to three miles and beyond, and are matched against rivals of a similar standard along the way. A business should nurture its leaders of the future with the same kind of careful progression.

Our future success will depend on finding inspirational leaders at every level. There are two big dangers: the failure to identify leadership potential; and promoting a future leader too quickly or to a job beyond their potential. Once promoted too far, it is difficult to put someone back into an appropriate role. (Although it's not impossible – we have four ex-area managers who now each run a shop, both happily and successfully.)

There is no secret formula: great leaders don't follow textbooks. It's not just a question of cutting costs, chairing meetings and making a few decisions. Good leaders display their personality, use their flair and lead by example. They gain respect by walking the job and listening to their team. They are particularly good at picking the right people to help them run the business. They make the rules, define the business boundaries and set the pace; in the process, they make it look simple.

Good leadership will always matter. Our upside-down management expects you to delegate most things – but never delegate strategy or hide your personality. The good news is that the leader gets most of the fun jobs – thinking for the business, making the big decisions and doing the deals. But you need to be self-motivated. Don't expect a lot of praise. Team members get the credit for success and the leader gets the blame when things go wrong.

When I can no longer play an active part in the business – which I hope will be some time away – there are several things I want to hand over to my successors: 100 per cent family control; a strong cash position; a good brand name; market leadership; plus loads of ideas to make the business even better.

These will provide a solid platform for further prosperity. But the most important legacy for future success is a strong management team. My top priority is to develop the next generation of leaders.

LESSONS

- Be determined to win
- Be patient
- Don't promote future stars too far, too quickly
- Display your personality
- Lead by example
- Walk the job
- Listen
- Pick the right people
- Delegate most things, but not strategy
- Make the big decisions

Chapter 14

DEAR JAMES REVISITED

❝We have introduced lots of ideas that work. We now need to understand what those ideas are ❞ James Timpson

I have just re-read my book *Dear James* for the first time since it was published seven years ago. The words were familiar. (After all, I had read the manuscript four times while working on it for three hours every morning during a holiday in Mustique.) No wonder I left it so long before picking up the book again. My intention was to bring the section on leadership up to date, but the world hasn't changed that much. So I have, with little alteration, reproduced the parts that matter most.

THE TOP JOB

Don't believe what you read in the newspapers. Running a business is not about big deals or being driven to the office by a chauffeur. You don't sit behind a desk making snap decisions and you shouldn't spend your life in meetings. Textbooks give useful guidelines, but there are no rules for an entrepreneur. Business schools don't tell you everything about being a chief executive; they provide the theory but not the practise. Read as many management books as you like, but take 80 per cent of your lessons from experience.

FAMILY BUSINESS TRAINING

A family business has two great advantages: a lifetime knowledge of the industry and the fact that you risk your own money. Managers trained by big companies sometimes assume an independent family business is run by a bunch of amateurs. In 1985, when our retail shoe business was going through a bad time, we recruited some senior managers from the Burton Group, the most successful retail company of that time. It was a disaster. The new recruits worked harder than anyone else, before or since. They used the techniques that made money at Burton, but they didn't work for Timpson.

SET THE STYLE

You set the style of the business, but you can't run a company without support from employees. Your job is to lead them. People want to know who they are working for. Once they recognise you as the boss, they will be guided by your expectations. Businesses often reflect the personality of their founder: Body Shop and Anita Roddick; Virgin and Richard Branson; Kwik Fit and Tom Farmer; Dixons and Stanley Kalms. These companies flourished by following the clear style set out by their first chief executive. Inspirational leaders are a hard act to follow, but a business always needs rare talent to galvanise success.

Your job is to define the main problems and find solutions that work. There are many possible strategies. You don't have to discover the perfect solution; you just choose one and stick with it. You think for the business and make the big decisions. You choose the overall direction, decide when to make changes and make change happen. It is no good having a great idea that doesn't become reality. You are the only person who can clear away the obstacles that get in the way. You will constantly face resistance to change. I wanted to introduce watch repairs in 1990 but, as we couldn't find a qualified watch repairer, it didn't happen. It was seven years before watch repairing resurfaced on the Timpson agenda. With more determination in 1990, we would have found a few watch repairers to launch the new service and by now would have a much bigger business. No one tried hard enough to find the watch repairers because I hadn't convinced our key people that it was the right thing to do.

THE RIGHT PEOPLE

You can't be in 630 shops at once, so you have to rely on your colleagues to run the business. It is not your job to do the detail. There are plenty of people who are better at repairing shoes than you. Your job is to pick people. Promote colleagues that demonstrate success – the winners, not the efficient administrator, the good talker or the person who looks smart but doesn't perform.

Make lots of internal appointments. Consistent success is created by gradual changes; businesses thrive on stability. When I was a shoe buyer, I worked with two of the most respected people in the industry. Tom Howell bought children's shoes and Tom Hardman purchased women's footwear. Both joined the business when they left school. As a business gets bigger, more graduates appear. Brains, though, are not the main qualification; look for personality and the ability to make things happen.

SET STANDARDS

Originally, our shoe repair factories were hidden from the public. When we put the shoe repair machinery on view in the 1970s, our operatives took the first step to becoming retailers. But their style was based on the factories of 1951, not the high street of 1971.

In 1979, during a week of branch visits, I realised the business lacked retail standards. The shops still looked like factories, shelves were dirty, staff had not shaved, there was an overflowing ashtray on the counter. I introduced some new rules: no smoking in the shop, no cups of tea on the counter, daily dusting of displays and a disinfected loo. The most important change was to insist men wore a tie. Ties became the symbol of our new retail standards; good housekeeping became part of the Timpson image.

Our outlets changed but the rest of the industry didn't seem to notice. Most independent shops are still just as scruffy. If you don't care whether standards are maintained, no one else will.

BEWARE THE BOX-TICKER

Don't be dominated by administrators. Left on their own, pen-pushers concentrate on saving money and writing rules that keep power concentrated at head office. You want a business that delegates authority to those who serve our customers.

COMMUNICATE

Everyone has the right to know what is going on and they need to hear it from the boss. The chief executive should listen to everybody and tell them everything. People like to know who they are working for; they want to meet him or her face to face. You cannot expect employees to trust a boss they only recognise from a name from the bottom of a memo. Your job is to listen, set the standards, get the thinking straight, tell everyone about it and give everyone the authority to get on and run the business for you.

GET THE THINKING STRAIGHT

When I was at university studying industrial economics, I couldn't understand why my tutor posed obvious questions: "What business are you in? What are you good at? And what things are most important in your business?" The answers seemed obvious. At that time, we were in the shoe business. We were good at selling shoes and it was important to have the right shoes in the right shops. Simple answers to obvious questions. I now ask myself the same questions that I heard at university. With no direct day-to-day responsibility, I can stand back and think about the future. You can be too close to your business; often the answer is staring you in the face. Most successful business plans are based on a heavy dose of common sense. They come with an inspirational flash of the obvious. You don't need genius, just a clear mind, but the outsider might think you are visionary.

KEEP IT SIMPLE

People can't understand complicated plans and as a result they don't work. Here is our current strategy:

We are a specialist service business selling merchandise relevant to the service we provide. Shoe repairs, although still important, is in long-term decline; to grow we must develop other services. We advertise by giving great customer care, which we achieve through upside-down management. We trust branch colleagues with the freedom to serve customers the way they think best. We recruit on personality and provide the training needed to turn raw recruits into craftsman. We look after our good people and recognise the vital role played by our area team. We will not expand outside the British Isles, so the core business will soon reach its full potential. We need to find new service businesses for future growth.

That's it – 119 words that get our thinking straight. You don't need consultants or market research but you do need to know the business. Ideas don't come to a desk; inspiration appears where you least expect it. Planning conference delegates sit round for hours without a single good thought between them. In the 1970s it was fashionable to disappear on forward-planning retreats at sun-drenched resorts, which supplied the space for new ideas. These expeditions can be dangerous. They often occur in response to poor trading and make matters even worse. Most inspiration lies within the business. You find it by visiting branches – you are unlikely to spot a winning wheeze by flying to a beach 1,000 miles from your nearest shop.

Our one-time competitor, Minit Solutions, was created by consultants and focus groups. It was a great theory: a range of services under one roof that could be turned into a global retail brand, but its creators had no practical experience. As a result, they built a business that did not work. It failed because their people lacked the skill to provide the services on offer.

We could have told them but their market research said something different. It was an expensive mistake. They lost £120m simply because decision-makers didn't understand their business.

IN A MEETING

I am wary of meetings. They seldom produce the answer to your problems. It is dangerous to make decisions at a meeting but they do have some uses. There are three good reasons for holding a meeting:

1. To tell people what is going on, such as James's monthly town hall meetings held at Timpson House to update everyone on site;
2. Meetings to monitor progress such as our board meetings; our eight times yearly forum to check up what's going on;
3. Meetings to discover new ideas, which we sometimes call a summit.

Summits are my favourite form of meeting. We gather together experts. We don't select participants by seniority; the management structure doesn't always indicate where the expertise lies. We aim for a group of around six people. At one summit, branch managers with the best watch repair turnover were asked how they did it. Their ideas probably put 20 per cent on total watch repair sales.

Discussions often go in unexpected directions. A group formed to discuss the future of computer engraving told us a lot about computers but the real benefit was more fundamental: they said our pricing structure was wrong. Engraving is time consuming and our prices were so low that some staff felt they earned a better bonus by concentrating on key cutting and shoe repairs. They were turning engraving business away. We increased engraving prices 20 per cent and sales went up 25 per cent.

HOLIDAY READING

The best business books are those written by entrepreneurs about real businesses. One day I hope to produce a website, www.businessbooksworthreading.com, with a list designed to help people avoid useless theory and direct them towards helpful practice.

Books that would be on my list include:

Boo Hoo: A refreshing story about the failure of Boo.com. It's a real page-turner that demonstrates how far a business can go before someone blows the whistle.

Maverick: Ricardo Semler's description of the amazing way he used democracy to run his business.

Nuts: The story of South West Airlines shows the single-minded way in which it promotes service to customers. This is an essential read for anyone who realises the importance of customer care.

The Nordstrom Way: This is the book that led me to upside-down management.

The Rise and Fall of M&S: Judy Bevan's well written account of how a great business can go off the rails.

The Richer Way: Julian Richer's commonsense approach to running a business.

All these books can give you ideas. But it is you, the leader, that must make them work.

ALWAYS KEEP A LIST

Do not expect your ideas to be welcomed with open arms. New ideas put people on the defensive. They resist change by producing a string of reasons to demonstrate why they will not work. I particularly remember an example of this at a Norvic shoe shop in Windsor, back in 1975.

We were starting a closing-down sale. The manager made a last-ditch attempt to hang on to his traditional values. Our closing-down sales had been so successful elsewhere that a queue formed before we opened. We did ten times a normal week's business in the first two days of every sale. To cope with the crowds, shoes were put on racks and the chairs were hidden behind the scenes.

Our Windsor manager was not happy. He could not contemplate selling shoes without providing a proper service – using shoehorns, sitting on the fitting stool and lacing shoes for the customer. "They will not like it in Windsor," he said.

"It has worked everywhere else," we responded.

"But they can't try on shoes without sitting down," he said with concern.

"The chairs will be in the way," we retorted.

Then came his final crushing argument. "What about the one-legged folk?"

We ignored him, cleared the chairs and filled the shop full of shoe racks. Windsor was very enthusiastic about our sale. By 9.30am, a large queue had formed under the shadow of Windsor Castle. At the front of the queue was a man with one leg.

Don't throw any ideas away. You never know when they might come in useful. Keep a list of all your brainwaves, even if other people think they are ridiculous.

THE BIG THINK

Have a private planning session every six months. Dig out all your lists and think. Ask yourself: "What is the easiest way to improve the business?" During a recent thinking session, I realised how much of our success was due to our area managers and the teams that support them. I wrote on my A4 pad: "Our future depends on our area teams." I sat for a while before adding: "Management training." That big think made field staff training my top priority. It gave me the determination to make management training work. We are well on the way to building a scheme which should help to ensure that we still have excellent area teams in 20 years' time.

VISITING SHOPS

One day I was in my study, planning my diary, when I realised Alex was looking over my shoulder.

"Lots of golf and tennis, I suppose?" she said. "You should be visiting more shops. As the father figure of our business you should talk to branch staff, not play games or sit in silly meetings."

"But," I protested, "in 18 months I've visited every branch."

"In that case," said Alex, "start all over again."

Last year I spent more than 100 days on the road. I've been touring the high street for 47 years. A month ago, I played golf with a guy who talked about his visit to our Bournemouth branch. He was amazed that our manager not only knew me but had met me several times.

"Have you got a helicopter?" he asked.

"I tried a helicopter once to visit Cornwall," I replied. "It saved travelling time, but it took a full day's planning to find both the friendly farmers who let us land on their fields and the taxi drivers to meet us."

When I saw the bill for our trip I was depressed for days. I do use a private plane instead of a scheduled airline but, normally, I travel by car, usually with a driver so I can do paperwork and be delivered to the shop door.

"Do they know that you're coming?" asked the golfer.

"If I go with an area manager, everyone is prepared," I replied, "but on my own I get in one surprise visit before the telephones start buzzing." (One day, after calling at Huddersfield, I arrived at a busy Bradford branch as the phone rang – so I answered it. "Just so you know," said the caller, "John Timpson is on his way.")

My golf pal had a final question. "What's your agenda? Do you have a checklist?"

"I don't look for trouble," I replied. "I'm not an inspector, so I go for a chat. It's normally trivia but, as a result, I know every shop from the front door to the lavatory."

My mind keeps an up-to-date picture of the high street in general and our competitors in particular. More importantly, I know something about our colleagues' holidays, hobbies, football teams and children.

It's amazing what you discover when you are not looking for anything. In one fortnight, I unearthed a serious staff shortage in Inverness, overstocking in Salisbury, a display problem in Newton Abbott and an opportunity to increase sales in Ipswich. I met an area manager with some great new training ideas and Brian, our manager in Aberdeen, who was celebrating his 50th birthday. Brian's shop was festooned with balloons but I was not happy – all our people have their birthday off but Brian had to work because he was short-staffed.

Occasionally I stumble on a big idea. Kelvin in Newport showed me how to add memorial plaques to our house sign business. In 1996, Glenn in West Bromwich preached the potential of watch repairs and persuaded me to give the new service a big push.

My visits remind me that managers know much more about their business than head office. That's why we let John Whelan design his own refit in Hammersmith and probably why he raised turnover by 20 per cent.

At a business dinner I met a man who uses our branch in Cirencester.

He was surprised that I knew the name of our manager, Bill Odell.

"You must travel a lot to know them so well," he said. "Doesn't your wife complain?"

"No," I said, "she pushes me out as she says it's the best way to run the business." As usual, Alex is absolutely right.

MAKE EASY DECISIONS

I wish I had read the next sentence 20 years ago. It would have saved time worrying about things that did not matter and decisions that I never made. Avoid difficult choices: just make the obvious decisions where you know the answer.

BEING PESTERED

A stream of people will pop into your office expecting you to make decisions. Cars create the biggest problem. Despite your carefully considered car policy, some people always want one that is better than their last one, or better than the guy in the next office or better than their next-door neighbour. They argue about savings on depreciation, about better miles per gallon and the lower servicing costs to justify the most expensive vehicle they think that you will allow.

Shop staff want snap decisions. "Can we close on Good Friday?" "Can you upgrade my key cutting machine?" "Can I advertise on the back of Sainsbury's receipts?" "My area manager says that I can't take four weeks off to see my daughter in South Africa – is that fair?" Avoid all these decisions. Don't undermine people with the real authority. Let your team make the decisions. Never take decisions on their behalf. Even when you see something needs to be done, never intervene.

BIG DECISIONS

Few decisions are crucial. I have only made ten that have made real differences to my career. The first was to ask Alex to marry me. Luckily, she said yes and has advised me on all subsequent major decisions.

Staying with UDS following their takeover of Timpson shows that ducking a decision can be the right option. Within two and a half years, my world turned round and I was the managing director of Timpson. One of my biggest decisions was the management buyout. It takes courage to challenge your boss and bid for the business. You know things will never be the same again. It took three months of careful thought to pluck up the courage.

A decision in 1985 to concentrate on key cutting provided a platform for our success. The idea came from a 30-minute conversation but it took ten years to develop the concept.

Selling our shoe shops in 1987 was clear logic overcoming emotional prejudice. Once I took a detached view, I saw that the odds were stacked against shoe retailing. But it still took six months to come to terms with the evidence before putting the shops up for sale. After selling them, I expected to have plenty of time for golf, tennis and holidays, but within four months we had made our first acquisition and shoe repair was becoming an obsession.

Alex made the next major decision. She told me never to float the company. She correctly forecast that I would never cope with the interference of analysts and stockbrokers. That made the next major decision almost inevitable. My fellow shareholders did not want to be locked into a private business, so I mortgaged our house for £1m, bought their shares and became the 100 per cent owner of the company.

Buying Automagic was a decision made in a hurry. We had been looking at the business for seven years but in receivership things move quickly. The receiver sold the business within three weeks. We had 12 hours to make our final bid.

Our decision to offer watch repairs has made a major difference and, with sales of over £12m, now looks an obvious move. But in 1996 few thought that customers would visit a cobbler to have their watch repaired.

The purchase of Minit in 2003 was another big decision. It was either courageous or foolish to buy a business that had lost £120m in four years, even for £1. The next 12 months were not easy. The Minit acquisition only fell into place when we sold Sketchley and SupaSnaps.

That's it. Ten important decisions in 47 years – and only one made in a hurry.

MAKE LIFE EASY

You can avoid most decisions through hard work. The more you know about your business, the easier decisions become. You know the right answer by instinct. These three rules will help you avoid difficult decisions.

- Delegate as many decisions as possible.
- Never take a decision unless you know the answer.
- Know the business so well that decisions, when necessary, are instinctive.

Avoiding decisions will reduce stress but don't be deceived. You can't duck decisions altogether. Your involvement is vital in the following areas.

CAPITAL PROJECTS

In our business, capital expenditure on branch refits and equipment such as computer engravers doesn't involve one big decision. You place several orders over many months. But board approval does not mean that the decision can't be changed. Keep everything under review.

PRODUCT DEVELOPMENT

A change to our products and services can have a profound effect. The introduction of watch repairs tipped the company's image from being dirty and artisan to a clean and skilful one.

Dry cleaning is a further move in the same direction. Minit's market research told them not to mix dirty shoe repairs with clean dry cleaning. So Minit Solutions hid shoe repair from the public and sales suffered. We don't need market research; we have the evidence of our own eyes. Dry cleaning and shoe repairs live happily side by side in many Johnson units, several of our London shops and our units in Sainsbury's. Instinct tells me the addition of dry cleaning is a good move. I agree with the Minit Solutions principles – the public will welcome a multi-service shop on the high street.

SMALL CHANGES THAT MAKE A DIFFERENCE

Don't delegate a decision just because it appears to be trivial. Some little things make a big difference.

The insistence that our staff wear ties had a significant effect on our branch image. Our "known as" list, with everyone's preferred Christian name or nickname, helps make our communications really personal. Banning voicemail made a major improvement to our service to branches – they no longer have to press buttons for the convenience of head office. They are all pretty trivial issues but they help to create our culture. None would have happened without my personal intervention.

NEW SHOPS AND ACQUISITIONS

Never delegate decisions that have long-term implications. When you acquire a new shop, the lease commits the company for many years. The shop fitting will cost £50,000. Acquisitions have an even bigger effect. It is not just the amount of money spent, as every acquisition will change the shape of the whole business.

TOP PEOPLE

Pick the top management yourself. Our business has lots of superstars who need the support of a superb team of senior executives.

CLEAR YOUR MIND

Whenever you have a difficult problem, make a list. Write down the reasons for and against. I made a list in 2003 when we wondered whether to sell Sketchley. I assembled my thoughts into two columns: plus and minus. This was the result:

Plus	Minus
New growth opportunity	Shops out of position
Well-known name	Properties dilapidated
	Poor morale
	Business losing money
	Lots of investment required
	Major training scheme needed
	We know little about dry cleaning
	Sales are down on last year
	We have other things to do

The list did the job. It would have been arrogant and pig-headed not to sell the business. It was an easy decision and one of the best we have made.

If you do have to make up your mind, don't do it on your own. You will need the help of your team to make it work. Get their support by involving them in the decision.

Be careful and avoid the connoisseurs of constructive criticism. Plenty of people will tell you why good ideas won't work – most people vote for the status quo. Here are just some of the reasons I was given for not trying watch repairs: customers don't associate us with watch repairs; there is too much competition; we haven't the skilled staff; our shops are too dirty; there is nowhere to secure watches overnight; we will never compete with the jewellers.

Despite all these reasons, watch repairs are a huge success. We had to win over the critics. Watch repairs were introduced gradually and each successful trial persuaded a few more people. Indeed, some critics now claim they played a vital part in developing this very successful new service.

If you meet really strong opposition – however good the idea – shelve it and go for something more popular with your team. Being a bit of a wimp makes for an easier life and can create a more successful business.

TAKE YOUR TIME

In an independent business, where the shareholders run the company, we can make very quick decisions. But don't be decisive and get the wrong answer. And don't let anybody hold you to a deadline. You can sleep on most decisions for weeks and, while you are waiting, new facts often emerge. It is not weak to be half-hearted. Test things in a small way. A trial to show whether the idea works often indicates how to do things better.

If your excellent idea is rejected by the team, keep planting the seed until someone else comes up with the idea. Your biggest critic may well claim the idea as their own. There are always three answers: yes, no and maybe. Doing nothing is often as courageous as changing your mind.

BIG DEALS

Our business has to grow. There is no choice. Standing still is not a strategy. To reach our current target of 900 shops and £20m profit, we must open several new shops and almost certainly need to make big and small acquisitions.

Don't open a shop unless you have seen the site at least twice. Get two other people to do the same. Computers can calculate the likely number of customers, based on social and economic groups and their spending power. I prefer to walk the high street and use the back of an envelope.

For years, our finance department insisted on producing a complicated appraisal for every new shop. They forecast five-year sales, calculated costs in detail and forecast the return using sophisticated discounted cash flows. The figures look so convincing that it is easy to forget they depend on your sales forecast. Today, I don't bother with computer modelling. I use two simple methods: first, I guess the weekly turnover and multiply by ten – if the answer is greater than the annual rent, we will make money. My other approach is to look at the branch accounts of an existing branch that most closely matches the proposed new unit.

I rely on instinct. After decades of walking the high street, you tend to know when a unit will work.

Things can go wrong. I got it wrong in Soho where I thought that a prominent corner site on Wardour Street, surrounded by sex shops and massage parlours, would work well. A lot of customers passed the door but there wasn't much demand for our sort of services. James took a chance in Torquay. The rent was quite high for a seaside town (my grandfather told me not to take a shop on the coast, because no one lives in the sea). Torquay struggled for its first 12 months. Maybe James regrets that he didn't ask for my opinion but, frankly, it would not have helped. When I saw the shop shortly after it had opened, I backed James's decision.

DON'T OVERPAY

In 1989 I nearly succumbed to the property boom. I was offered a group of six shops for a premium of £150,000. They were all prime sites and I could only see success. But the shops were too big and the rent was too high. Fortunately, I pulled out. If the deal had gone ahead, I would have lost a lot of sleep and loads of money.

We can't compete against the latest fast-growing retailer. We have been outbid by coffee bars, juice bars and mobile phone shops. We have seen rents inflated by jeans retailers, sock shops and tie businesses rolling out their concepts. Their agents, with requirement lists that cover all the prime locations, are willing to pay whatever price it takes to get the unit. When their new concept ceases to be the flavour of the month, high rents can kill the company. Even if you fall in love with the property, never pay more than it is worth.

CLOSING TIME

We close up to ten branches a year, whether we like it or not. Ends of leases, relocations and redevelopments at first appear unwelcome. In retrospect, however, they keep the business up to date. We also close loss-making shops. We don't rush to close units; it takes five years to establish a shop and only five minutes to shut it. So before committing to closure, there are four questions:

- Would a star manager turn it round?
- If a competitor closed, would that transform the business?
- Is the difficulty short term, such as road works or car parking?
- If we acquired a multiple competitor and this shop was part of their portfolio, would we keep it?

Unless the answer is "no" to each of these questions, let the shop stay open and think again in 12 months.

ACQUISITIONS

Acquisitions help you grow quickly. Buying Automagic increased our business from 210 to 320 shops overnight. Within two years our turnover doubled. It doubled again when we bought Minit. We have been very lucky. So far, every purchase has matched our profit expectations. As with the golfer Gary Player, the more you know about the industry, the more luck you get finding the next acquisition.

Doing deals can be fun. It's the glamorous part of the job. Accountants love them – it's their equivalent of playing in a cup final or a test match. Lawyers thrive on deals and merchant banks depend on them but, be warned, although deals give a big buzz, they don't always work.

The purchase of SupaSnaps blew Sketchley off course. Instead of helping its dry cleaning business, SupaSnaps brought more problems. Minit's purchase of Sketchley was even more disastrous.

Before starting negotiations, ask these questions:

1. Does it fit in with our strategy?

The buzz of a deal is so attractive that it is tempting to get involved with anything on offer. We get regular approaches from people who think that our concept would be successful elsewhere in the world. They may be right, but expansion overseas is not for us. It is not part of our strategy.

2. Are you sure it will increase profits?
Only do deals where success is a near certainty. You have to see a clear way to create cash and increase profits. When we buy a competitor, we want the shops but not their head office. In that way, branch contributions go straight to our bottom line. More than £500,000 of Automagic's overheads rapidly disappeared after we bought them; profits had to go up. With Minit, the savings were more than £3m.

3. Do you know how to run it?
You must have a plan. Get your thinking straight for the new business before you negotiate. Have a picture in your mind – both for the first ten weeks and first 12 months – before you make an offer. After completion, talk to your new colleagues, as they will help with the details and strengthen your strategy.

4. Who will run it?
Keep an open mind about the people you acquire. You will find lots of talent – one third of our area managers joined us as a result of acquisitions. But don't delegate the day-to-day running of the business to someone you do not know. Appoint a general manager and finance controller who you know well. You can trust them to establish your style of management in the new business. We take our culture for granted but it will be difficult to explain to others. You must have your own man in charge.

5. Why are you doing it?
An acquisition may provide an easy and relatively risk-free route to growth, but are you sure it is worth the hassle?

6. What is the risk?
Profit has been defined as the reward for taking risks. That is misleading. Risk should be avoided whenever possible. Profits can be made from racing certainties. Never risk the existing business.

7. Is the current business OK?

Acquisitions take more time than you can ever imagine. Don't get involved without a good accountant, a clever lawyer and lots of patience. If I go for a week without visiting any of our branches, I feel out of touch. Before contemplating a major acquisition, you must have confidence to leave day-to-day control to your management team while you are distracted by the deal.

FROM A HANDSHAKE TO COMPLETION

Buying a business takes longer than you think. It's not as simple as buying a car or even a house. It is an assault course with a predictable pattern. Many of the stages seem unnecessary, although accountants and lawyers might not agree. Once negotiations start, they play the leading parts and you only appear on stage from time to time as an extra.

Don't be nervous about approaching possible targets. If you don't ask, you may never do any deals. But be nice about it. I regularly receive approaches for Timpson, usually from arrogant figure-minded administrators in public companies who don't understand independent entrepreneurs. They think there is a price that I can't refuse. If there was one, their attitude would encourage me to sell to someone else.

You almost always approach your target at the wrong time. Even so, strike up a dialogue and sow seeds for later. The first encouraging sign is a confidentiality letter but, beware, lawyers will now be involved – and someone is paying their fee. Your finance director will ask his opposite number for information. He will ask for so much that it will take at least ten days to get a response. If it is shops you are buying, get a branch list ahead of the accounts so that you can start going round the business. Take lots of pictures and note your first impressions. When the numbers arrive, the computer takes over. Don't be deceived by random numbers – you can prove anything with figures.

Put yourself in the vendor's shoes. What are they thinking? What is important? What will make them happy? It takes two to make a deal. You need to agree, so don't be too clever. While we talked to Hanson about our buy-out in 1983, Burton was negotiating to buy Richard Shops and John Collier. Burton's chief executive Ralph Halpern took a tough line. Every time Hanson thought he had a deal, Halpern found a reason to drop the price. He did it once too often and Hanson broke off negotiations. He sold Richard Shops to Terence Conran's Storehouse and he sold John Collier to the management.

When you finally agree the heads of terms, there is still a long way to go. You have given a signal to your lawyers to crank up their word processors and bury you in paper (there is no way you can read this stuff on a computer screen). Lawyers can make enemies out of the best of friends. Some solicitors see life as a professional point-scoring exercise. As well as battling on your behalf, they want to beat the opposing legal firm. Clarify fees at an early stage; if costs are the last item discussed before contracts are exchanged, it could be expensive. Set a deadline. Lawyers will always find legal points to discuss. If they are charging an hourly rate, then the longer the deal, the larger the bill. The reason for a deadline doesn't matter – financial year end, holidays, Christmas – all can be used to end the talking and get the contract signed.

When the accountants have finished producing random numbers, and the lawyers have discussed their final point of principle, you will be left to run the business. It is then you realise how much thinking time has been taken up with the deal. The adrenalin flows for months – and then suddenly you recognise the pressure. You will never want to do a deal again. But acquisitions are the easiest way to grow. It will not be long before you are looking for another deal.

LESSONS

- Pick the key managers yourself
- Whenever possible promote from within
- Make sure everyone in the business knows you
- Don't be dominated by administrators
- Avoid difficult decisions
- Don't make decisions at a meeting
- Involve your team before making any decisions
- Have a solitary thinking session every six months
- Put pros and cons on paper before making up your mind
- Avoid risk whenever possible
- Never stop looking for ideas
- Always keep a list of things to do
- The better you know the business, the luckier you become

Chapter 15

BREAK
THE RULES

"When you threw out the EPOS system it gave the right message " Paul Masters

We don't like rules. We run the business using trust and respect. We gain a great advantage by giving our people the freedom to use their initiative. We don't need administrators to monitor targets or police the rules. We have time to watch our people carefully, correct their mistakes and learn from their ideas.

However big you get, act like a small business. You will never need a strategy director or a controller of corporate communications. If you delegate these vital roles, you lose control of the business. Central strategy is your job. That includes leading a personal crusade against red tape.

Challenge everything. Someone, somewhere, is producing a report that nobody will read. Someone else is spending money to comply with regulations that don't apply to us. When we acquired Sketchley in 2003, I was given a mound of paperwork proudly produced by their EPOS system. It analysed merchandise sales. It gave sales breakdowns by day, by price, by colour and anything else you could imagine. Three young graduates had enthusiastically analysed the information at head office, apparently unaware that the business was losing £3m each year and fast running out of cash. Some companies rely too much on intelligent graduates with complete faith in computer data. It's often wiser to employ ordinary folk with charisma and common sense.

Following a visit to our shop in Kendal where I saw a hearing-aid system – our response to a report from the Disability Rights Commission – I started to notice every recent shop refit incorporated the device.

"How much is it?" I asked.

"We did a good deal," came the reply.

"That does not answer my question," I insisted. "How much does is cost?"

"We got it down to £45 per branch," I was told.

"Why do we need them?" I continued.

"It's a legal requirement."

A few weeks later, James asked me to redraft a letter. Apparently we had to write to the parents of 16- and 17-year-olds to explain that their child was working with dangerous machinery. It was a new government requirement and had something to do with age discrimination. I looked at the draft letter. I could see why James was worried:

Dear Parent,

I am writing to let you know that your son/daughter who has applied to join our company will be working with dangerous machinery. Key cutting and shoe repairs involve the use of high-speed cutters and fast-moving abrasive wheels. Although we have guards, accidents can happen. Your son/daughter will be given health and safety training before they are allowed to use any machinery and we have rules that cover the wearing of protective clothing and goggles. We will do everything possible to look after your son/daughter while he/she is in our workplace and we are covered by insurance for any injury claim. However, you should be aware of the dangers associated with working in our trade.

I thought the message could be put across more tactfully but decided first to look up the relevant legislation. I discovered there is an obligation to tell parents about risk in the workplace – but only for children under 16. The only 15-year-olds who work in our shops are children of employees gaining work experience.

My mind went back to the hearing aid issue. I looked up the legislation covering disabled access. The compulsory provision of hearing aids is not in the Act; it is only vaguely mentioned in a guideline produced by a consultant. As a result of these discoveries, I took a new approach. If the legal requirements seem silly, I look at the legislation. If ignoring the guidelines can't make me a criminal, I follow my instinct and stick to common sense.

The management team needs your respect but don't be afraid to cut across the management structure. In businesses where internal politics are top of the agenda, everyone is well aware of their place in the pecking order and are wary of anything that undermines their authority. Everything is communicated through the chain of command. The attendance of meetings is determined by seniority. Senior managers get a copy of every memo. Don't pander to these business politics. Walk round the office and talk to everybody, especially those in the front line. Listen to the gossip and feel free to barge into someone else's meeting.

It is not easy to run a business by relying on trust and common sense. The business world is so committed to dictatorial management, you will be pulling against a strong urge to return to the comfort of rigid structure and rules. Our way is unusual. It is not taught in business schools that train professional managers. It is not helped by government legislation, which assumes everything is controlled from the centre. You must show leadership by supporting the mavericks who break the rules and show initiative.

Alex Barrett (whom we met in an earlier chapter), has a style of his own. After he had been promoted to regional manager, I visited his old area and asked my usual questions.

"Have you any problems? How's the area team?"

"I had a problem and it has been dealt with, but not in the way Alex would have done it," said one manager.

"Tell me more," I said.

"I had a spot of bother at home. My partner and I had a few difficulties and it affected my work. I turned up late on a few occasions and received counselling and an oral warning. I understand all that, it's the new system. My area manager says that he has to follow the procedure laid down by employment law.

"When I had problems years ago, Alex took me in the back of the shop and told me not to be so bloody stupid. In five minutes he gave me the straightest talk I have ever had in my life and I got the message."

Alex gets my backing. He knows how to play the game: he doesn't ignore the rules but he bends them to get the result. If you allow people to break the rules in the cause of common sense, they will create better displays, invent new services and go well beyond their terms of employment for the good of the business. Take the team at our concession in Sainsbury's in Gloucester who, during the floods in July 2007, had no water to operate their dry-cleaning machine. For a week, they took everything to Swindon and worked through the night so that customers would not be disappointed. That doesn't happen when people are trained to stick to the rules.

It's your job to question everything. Don't accept advice from people who say "you can't do that". We have a help desk; it was set up when we bought Minit. To handle the large number of calls, an answerphone was installed. "It's the only way we can cope," I was told.

Staff rang in from busy shops, often with customers waiting, but nobody answered the phone. "Every other office has voicemail," it was said. But I banned it. Today every call is answered by a real person. It's often

Dorys, who looks after our switchboard, and she knows a lot of branch managers by the sound of their voices. Nearly four years later, I hear nothing but good reports about our service from branch colleagues. Nobody at Timpson House has ever asked me to restore the voicemail.

We are relatively free from red tape because we don't apply for any government subsidies but, from time to time, I wonder whether we are missing out. After all, the government distributes lots of money to industry and it could be a way to get some of our tax back. I was reminded of this thought one day when I heard the prime minster say that thousands of businesses were benefiting from the New Deal. "Under this government everyone wins – workers, employees and the tax payer," he blustered.

It made me think, because we were not a New Deal winner. I spoke to Peter, our training manager. Peter winced when I mentioned New Deal.

"Do you want the full story?" he asked, hoping that I hadn't time.

"Go ahead," I said. "Tell me all about it."

"Can I start with NVQs?" asked Peter.

"If you insist," I replied. In 1990 I had attended several NVQ meetings with a group of drearily dressed *Guardian* readers from a training centre in Sheffield, three hard-pressed independent cobblers and some others who had travelled a long way, then said very little and completed expense forms. These terrible, tedious meetings eventually bored me into resignation.

"I took your place on the committee," said Peter. "Three years and 20 meetings later, the Shoe Repair Industry Training Organisation (SRITO) launched its NVQ for shoe repairs. Sadly, SRITO was seriously underfunded. So, finding you in a fit of altruism, I persuaded you to buy SRITO and to give me responsibility for shoe repair NVQs. I am proud that, in 18 months, it helped 70 people gain the new qualification."

"Well done, Peter," I said. "But you don't run SRITO now. Did you lose interest?"

"They changed the rules," he replied. "ITOs were replaced by National Training Organisations. These were larger and more efficient. We had to join with other trades. We objected strongly. We sent out 18 copies of a 300-page report and complained to our local MP. It made no difference. Cobblers were classed with tanners and shoe-makers, neither of whom understood shoe repairs and key cutting. It's getting worse. NTOs could become even bigger. We might be joined by textile workers, saddlers and veterinary surgeons. Our training advisers won't know a heel from a horse's hoof."

"So you lost interest in NVQs?" I persisted.

"It's fair to say NVQs lost interest in us," replied Peter, "as our industry was too small to fit into their master plan. NVQs might be good for some sectors but they didn't work for us. Mind you," he continued, puffing out his chest, "it gave us time to concentrate on our own scheme, which I modestly suggest has been a great success. Eighty-seven per cent of our employees say our training is good or very good."

"Well done again Peter, but what has this to do with New Deal? Why aren't we one of the winners from it?"

"Simple," said Peter. "They wouldn't let us join. Every New Deal employee has to take an NVQ. We preferred our own training, which does everything that NVQs do and a lot more besides. The New Deal unit studied our scheme for 18 months but still said no."

"Why couldn't they extend NVQs to everything we do?" I asked.

"That needed a new joint-funded project," Peter explained.

"You mean they wanted our money?" I added.

"No, not money," corrected Peter, "our time and expenses. Anything connected with the project, particularly travelling, would count as our contribution to the new module."

"So," I said, "the more we spend on expenses, the more they like it. Perhaps that's why so many training managers travel first class."

Peter looked perplexed. "But businesses only cover 51 per cent of the project cost."

"So," I asked, "who pays the other 49 per cent?"

"The government," said Peter. "They spend it on consultants."

I started to understand. "You mean the more time and money we spend, the more government can pay consultants?"

"That's right," said Peter.

"Would it be cynical," I suggested, "to say that consultants get paid because we spend time and money travelling to tell them all about our business so they can tell the civil servants who can then tell us what to do?"

"Got it," said Peter. "That's why I thought it better to use our own training scheme and forget about NVQs. I am sorry that, in the process, Timpson failed to be a New Deal winner."

I clearly didn't look convinced.

"Not happy?" asked Peter. "I will give you some homework." He produced a pile of NVQ paperwork that ruined my next weekend. I started with the 1997 report on occupational mapping in the shoe repair industry. This concluded: "We should proceed to review and develop relevant NVQs to cater for shoe repairing, key cutting and engraving. The award should be constructed with common mandatory core and function-specific optional units."

By Monday morning I was familiar with NVQ terminology – key competencies, performance objectives, knowledge requirements.

"A lot of it is gobbledegook," I told Peter when we next met.

"You don't understand," said Peter. "All NVQs are like that. It's their standard format."

I was bemused. "You mean there is a special way that NVQs are written?"

"Yes," said Peter.

"Do I detect scope for an NVQ for people who write NVQs?" I asked.

"For goodness' sake, don't tell them that," said Peter, "or they will call in another consultant."

My faith was restored at a dinner for companies that had been listed by the *Sunday Times* as great places to work. I quizzed a big retailer who was high on the list.

"How many of your people are involved in NVQs?" I asked.

"None," she replied. "We concentrate on in-house training. Our employees like it."

When I next saw Peter, I apologised. "I now understand why we aren't a New Deal winner. Incidentally, how much did the footwear NVQ cost?"

"If you include money spent by the industry, consultants and the Training Agency, you will be close to £2m," said Peter.

"Final question, Peter. How many shoe repairers are currently following an NVQ?"

Peter smiled as he replied. "Two."

It's a good indication that some of the most expensive and time-consuming legislation comes from the world of personnel and training. Fortunately, we have our own training scheme but, when it comes to personnel, our associate director in charge of people support is particularly keen that we understand the rules.

Following his suggestion, I signed on for a day's conference called Driving Business Results Through People Strategy. I was surrounded by HR executives. "We live in a challenging world," said the keynote speaker. "We need to come up with strategies that are owned by each stakeholder. Everyone must use 360-degree vision to become more customer-facing. It's about getting out of the box and aspiring to become an entrepreneurial business focused on delivery 24/7."

Keen delegates took notes. Others started to play buzzword bingo. But HR people are guilty of far worse than boring buzzwords. They are party to the plot that some call gold-plating. The problem starts with an EU Directive. A simple new regulation described by Brussels in 100 words is turned by Whitehall into 250; the supporting guidelines are four times as long. Then the HR professionals take over. Papers are written, seminars are held and best practice is developed. Within months, a simple rule is turned into a code of practice that the HR world regards as legally binding. That's when they say: "If you don't follow best practice, you won't have a leg to stand on at a tribunal."

These professional advisers thus add a new layer of rules that have never been passed by the EU or Westminster. The nanny state doesn't need to make new laws – they could just sit back and let professionals and consultants do the nannying for them. These codes and guidelines are getting so much credibility that some tribunals come down on people whose only crime is a failure to follow this gold-plated advice.

For us, this came to a head when we had to re-organise our central office following the sale of Sketchley and SupaSnaps. Sadly, there had to be redundancies. What was more appalling was that the personnel department insisted that everyone was told they were "at risk". I should never have let it happen. We sent letters to people who had been with us for over 25 years. They were not only among our most loyal employees but also my close friends. To suggest they were at risk of redundancy was a blatant lie. Our HR adviser, however, said that we had to hide the truth to avoid a possible tribunal.

Never again will I break trust, built over so many years, to satisfy some small print in a personnel consultant's guidebook. I will be guided by fairness and common sense rather than by government directives. I will ensure that entrepreneurs run the business, not personnel. I will never again allow loyal, long-service employees to be used as pawns to satisfy a procedural paper chase. I might lose the odd tribunal, but I will win the moral high ground and restore the respect of my workforce.

It is unfair to say that it's just personnel people who lay down the law. Usually finance has the most power, which they exercise through the budget. Budgets have little to do with running a business. They are good at controlling expenses. They provide a sound basis of communication with the bank manager. But, if you really want to measure results, don't bother with performance against budget and ignore KPIs. For a real test, compare with last year.

Although your bank manager may be satisfied with the management accounts, don't be deceived yourself. Accounts are riddled with so many estimates, provisions and contingencies that they cannot be trusted. Every day, I compare our bank balance with the same day last year. Cash in the bank is pure fact, untampered by the art of accountancy. The daily balance is your business barometer.

I don't hire consultants, except for specialist jobs such as PR and energy saving. I don't want marketing advisers or market researchers to tell me about our business. I prefer to keep my business knowledge up-to-date by visiting shops and talking to colleagues. I have always found it better to write my own agenda.

In 1998 I was invited to talk to a cobblers' conference in Guernsey. I knew shoe repairing was in decline but many operators had their heads in the sand. I decided to give it to them straight. I showed a series of graphs, charting the decline of the industry. My figures revealed that 65 per cent of the market would disappear in 15 years. Delegates became so worried that they didn't notice the words at the bottom of every chart: Source: Imaginary Research Ltd. I hadn't been able to find any statistics or information about our industry so I just made the figures up.

Three weeks later, I received a call from the *Financial Times*.

"I understand you have some facts about the shoe repair industry," said the journalist.

"Sort of, but I made them all up."

"That's a pity," he replied. "I have to write about your trade and yours are the only figures I can find. If you don't mind, I am going to use them."

A vivid imagination can be almost as good as market research. And it comes at a much cheaper price! Sitting in a doctor's waiting room a few months later, I compiled a shoe industry fact sheet. It revealed that people in Swansea and Glasgow have the smallest feet in Britain, while the biggest feet are found in Plymouth. The press release that included these fictitious "facts" was issued on a quiet news day. Camera crews were despatched to Plymouth, Swansea and Glasgow. The national newspapers – from *The Sun* to *The Times* – gave us the free publicity that we were seeking.

We tell our employees they must be 100 per cent honest but there are times when you should tell a lie for a good cause. Take business plans. Banks prefer figures to flair; they need something to stick into the computer to carry out sensitivity analyses. Everyone knows business plans are the extrapolation of dreams but, as long as your numbers show sales rising faster than costs, there is every chance the bank will lend you the money.

These lies save time. Be warned, though: if lies are so useful, other people will be lying to you. Few of us admit how often we are taken in by clever salesmen. Most of us believe what we read in the newspapers. Every day, we receive loads of false information, much of it disguised as official statistics. Governments don't lie – they spin. I invent facts to explain the truth, while the government uses real facts to create a false impression.

It is advisable to know your business inside out before you start inventing stories. So long as your fictitious facts back up the truth, you will create a happy workplace with an open and honest environment.

Our annual attitude survey asks how well we communicate. Over the years, we have developed such a reputation for free and frank information that one employee suggested we should tell everyone the facts behind any rumour before it starts going round the office. Our most recent employee survey showed how much employees appreciate the way we reveal all the facts, proving that a little bit of spin and a sprinkling of white lies are good for business. This, of course, might be another home truth produced by Imaginary Research Ltd. Here is another fact: the business will be more successful if you have the courage to break the rules in the interests of common sense.

LESSONS

Questions for a rule-breaking maverick

■ **Is the rule backed by the law?**

YES	NO	
■ What are the consequences of breaking the law?	**Who has created the lawful impression?**	
	a)	A "professional" – lawyer, accountant, consultant
■ Will you get caught?	b)	The media
■ What is the penalty?	c)	One of your own departments – HR, health & safety, finance, other
■ Is it worth it?		

■ **Do you strongly believe in common sense?**
■ **Do you want to break the rules?**
■ **Have you got the time and determination to overrule the rule-makers?**

Chapter 16
BE PARANOID

❝Keep doing the simple things – do what matters most❞ Kit Green

I came across this job advertisement in the *Sunday Times*.

Head of Contact Excellence

A leading global leisure player with diversified portfolio is experiencing rapid growth in product width and customer contact methodologies, which demand a top-notch individual reporting to the Director of Contact Centre Operations to drive customer contact management and deliver enhanced operational and service standards across five sites.

The successful candidate will be able to define, implement and monitor world-class service delivery standards at all points of interaction, and will have the experience to develop and roll out conversion strategies of individual customer segments which maximise sales and will also have the ability to benchmark contact handling abilities and customer delivery internally and externally.

They will be required to ensure best-in-class practice is shared across contact centres through the creation and management of excellence environments. We are looking for a candidate of graduate calibre, a senior management contact centre professional who is recognised as a sales/service guru with hands-on experience of contact centre and contact monitoring technology, offering diverse blue-chip B2C experience.

The candidate must be able to provide evidence of demonstrable success in developing benchmark processed and competency models, expertise in devising and managing learning and development solutions and will be a strategic thinker with a commercial action-orientated approach, and a natural leader, motivator and coach, with the ability to challenge perceptions and build strong relationships across a multi-site environment.

What's all that about?

If I am not looking for a top-notch individual who can monitor world-class delivery standards at all points of interaction, who do I want? I want someone who has "got it".

I want people with the determination to fight against the magnetic force that attracts most people to rely on the traditional control-and-command style of management. We need Jekyll and Hyde characters – the sometimes pessimist who is capable of inspiring the troops by being a perennial optimist. I want someone who is paranoid, never complacent. I want someone who encourages the business to celebrate success but is always worried what will happen next. I want someone who checks the cash every day. Every drop in turnover should be reason to visit the business to find out why. I want someone who knows the business so well that, when they visit the shops on a fact-finding tour, they discover the truth.

We suffered in April and May 2007. Sales were only just beating the previous year. James and I went to visit lots of shops. Although we discovered some examples of poor housekeeping and a few clear instances of poor management, we decided the only problem was the weather: summertime heat had come in early spring. When the temperature dropped and the rain came tumbling down in June and July, we showed a massive 15 per cent increase.

Often a blip in business reflects normal monthly fluctuations but it is still wise to be paranoid. Expect the unexpected. In 2004 our watch repairs, which had been consistently shooting up by an annual 25 per cent, suddenly stopped growing. It was many weeks before we realised the cause. Demand had fallen due to a change in watchstrap fashion from leather to metal straps, which last a lot longer. Until then, we hadn't realised that fashion had any influence on watch repairs.

You also get some nice surprises. There are new ideas such as the development of our photo ID business (helped by changes in passport regulations) and the introduction of our lifetime guarantees for both shoe repairs and watch batteries. These good ideas will only be spotted if you have an open mind.

Paranoia is not the same as prejudice. Mike Strom would never have lost his Automagic business if he had been positive about key cutting.

I want humble realists who are willing to admit mistakes. Saying sorry is one of the best ways to gain respect from your workforce. It's such a powerful management tool; it's almost worth making deliberate mistakes to give you the chance to apologise. You are never as good as you thought you were in your proudest moment. I want someone who is convinced they can always do better.

During the leadership course that James and I run, we ask area team members two questions: Which are the five poorest-performing branches in your area? How much more money would those branches take if you were running them?

The results are quite startling. They tell us that, simply by having a good manager in each of their shops, an area team could take an extra £4,000 per week. If that happened nationwide, company takings would increase by over £85,000 and annual profits would go up by £2.5m. It's a simple exercise that shows we can always do better.

Great leaders are never satisfied. Every record is there to be broken. People with ambition aim to earn success again and again. Plenty of companies have two or three good years; great companies have two or three good decades.

I want leaders who never accept mediocrity: "Okay" is not okay. "I suppose it will do" won't do. Perfection is where everything we do is the best. It's an impossible aim but a great catalyst for improvement.

I want leaders who are willing to invest in the future but are tight-fisted when controlling day-to-day expenditure. Lazy people can overpay because they can't be bothered to look for a better deal. Cost-cutting is an art, not a science. Look under every stone as James and Paresh did when they hid away for a day at James's home, looking at every invoice paid during the past 12 months. Such a detailed approach will show you the useless expenditure, which can then be eliminated without anybody noticing.

Here is the challenge: in every business, up to ten per cent of expenditure is wasted. The art is to save money without affecting performance. Never cut out costs that have a direct effect on turnover.

Everyone needs a guru – someone to talk to in times of trouble and a sounding board for big decisions. The guru could be a close and trusted colleague or a non-executive director.

To be successful, our leaders need the respect of their team. That doesn't always mean being Mr Nice Guy. A business is not a democracy. You call the big decisions; sometimes you have to disagree with your team. Don't buckle under their pressure but remember that you will need them on your side to get the ideas to work.

Be paranoid. Only take calculated risks. If in doubt, don't do it. Make up your mind slowly but, when you have decided what to do, do it straightaway.

That's the long form of my job advertisement. Here is the short version:

Timpson seeks a paranoid personality who relies on common sense.
- *A permanent pessimist with an open mind*
- *A perennial optimist who can admit mistakes*
- *A dedicated delegator with the courage to take big decisions*
- *A mean eye for cost control, but generous at handing out praise*
- *A stickler for standards who loves new ideas*
- *Knows how to celebrate success, but always aims to do better*

In short, we want someone who has "got it".
Big shots and empire builders need not apply.

Chapter 17

BE ECCENTRIC AND CREATE THE BUZZ

We like the fact that you are always looking for the next idea, keeping the buzz in the business Darren Brown

Last year, my credit card was rejected in Somerfield's small supermarket in Uppingham. I waited 30 minutes before the store managers could obtain authorisation for my payment. I contacted a NatWest call centre for card-holders. The man who answered was unhelpful, so I decided to complain.

"Could I have the name of your chief executive?" I asked.

"I don't know who it is," he replied. "The only boss I know is the woman who runs my section of the call centre."

You can't run a business if the business doesn't know who you are. You are the conductor of an orchestra; you don't play an instrument but the players expect you to set the tempo and create the excitement. But don't put on an act and play at being the big boss. Be yourself, display your emotions, share your joys and disappointments and, most of all, be visible. Don't spend every day behind a desk. If you have too much paperwork, put it in the bin.

You are the internal PR department; it's your job to meet everybody. Be as eccentric as you like. Talk to yourself out loud, wear colourful shirts and a cheerful face. A miserable-looking boss undermines confidence. Delegate all day-to-day problems to your team, so you have plenty of time to get round the business. But you must never delegate communication.

Don't let the training department, personnel or marketing be the first to tell the business what is going on. The workforce wants to hear it from you. You need to be a journalist, public speaker and media presenter. Tell everyone everything: sales, profit, cash flow, future plans and past failures. Only keep secrets dictated by data protection, personal privacy and confidentiality letters.

People find false reasons for keeping things confidential: "If they saw our profit increase, they would want a pay rise"; "It will get leaked to our competitors"; "Announcing bad results will affect morale". In 20 years, none of these fears have turned into reality at Timpson.

Competitors are more interested in bad news. If they hear we are doing better than them, they don't believe it. Everyone has a right to know how their business is performing. If times are good, employees should share in the success and get a big enough bonus to keep them happy.

Communicate strategy in a way that makes it memorable; you want everyone to know the direction you are heading and believe in it. Your job is to win their hearts and minds. Take time to get your message across. You won't change everyone's thinking with one memo; repeat the message month after month, year after year. Give pet projects a name. We use "Perfect Day" for our annual tidy-up campaign.

I don't go in for mission statements. Most are the cold product of a committee and have little relationship with reality. But the tag line on our fascia, "The Quality Service People", helped us focus on customer care. We have an even stronger message for the future – "Great Service from Great People".

We use lots of ways to say the same thing: DVDs, the front page of the weekly newsletter, the Timpson Calendar, staff room posters, the annual report to employees and, best of all, a hand-written message sent to everyone's home.

Keep going on about your strategy until colleagues realise it is not just flavour of the month or even this year's campaign. It is the way you want the business to be – forever. Just in case you haven't got the message, it is you that will be doing the communicating. You will speak to everyone – not just to senior and middle management but to everyone.

Don't delegate communication. Prepared scripts, cascading down the organisation, don't do the job. Your colleagues want to hear the message from you.

A hand-written personal letter from the chief executive of a 630-shop chain to one of 1,650 employees is time well spent. If possible, find a good reason for writing to 20 colleagues every month; it will make a massive impression. Hand-written letters are one of the most powerful tools at your disposal.

Most of your letters will say "well done". Praise is a vital part of leadership. We ask area managers to praise branch staff ten times as much as they criticise. That ratio also applies to the big boss. There are plenty of other ways to praise. A surprise phone call, a bottle of champagne delivered to home and a mention in the newsletter are all appreciated. But the most welcome way to say "well done" is money. Our bonus scheme rewards success every week but a special bonus makes a big impact.

I am a trustee of Uppingham School. It is a well-run, successful organisation. There is a waiting list and a recent inspection report was superb. We decided to do something almost unheard of in the world of education. We gave every member of staff (both academic and support) a £300 tax-paid bonus and sent them the first-ever trustees' report, saying who we are, what we do, and why we do it. The letters of thanks from Uppingham staff demonstrated that praise with an element of surprise is as welcome in a school as it is in a company.

I heard of one chief executive who thinks that praise is so important that he takes six pebbles on his daily walk around the factory. Every time he says "well done", he transfers a pebble pocket from his left pocket to his right. Every senior manager should have a discipline to keep up the level of praise. I put aside £1,000 per month to give to people who have done something exceptional. For a business making £12m, £12,000 a year is nothing.

As well as being communicator-in-chief, you are the entertainment officer. Encourage the business to celebrate success by having fun. Give people special occasions to look forward to and great parties to remember: award ceremonies, football tournaments, company birthday parties, an annual golf championship, or the office barbecue.

On the big occasions, you're the host. But in a business of our size, there are so many parties that you don't need to go to them all. The area booze-up is much better without you, but still fund half the cost and write to congratulate the organisers of a successful party.

We let our colleagues choose their own job titles. You can see them on their name badges: John "Chief Talker"; Jenny "The Expert"; Trevor "Customer Champion". I met two business leaders recently who have invented new titles for themselves: Richard Reed at Innocent Drinks calls himself the "Chief Squeezer"; Clare Owen at S G Group has the title of "Leader of Vision & Values". I would be happy to be called "Champion of Common Sense".

Give people lots of latitude to have fun. Let them decorate the shop to celebrate their birthdays (or even the shop's birthday) and create individual displays. For months, Doug Rimmer put his joke of the day in the shop window at Gillingham for the benefit of passers-by.

Accountants and cost-cutters may say these things have little to do with running a business and are a waste of money. How wrong can you get? It's your job as the eccentric leader to protect the company from dull killjoys who think business is only about rules and balance sheets. It's quirky things that create the buzz. It's your job to encourage extroverts to show their true colours.

We have five holiday homes, raise £20,000 each month for Childline, and publish an annual "Who's Who" with a picture and description for every employee. None of these things has much to do with repairing shoes or cutting keys but they make a big difference.

Few companies would spend £80,000 a year on their newsletter; few would have enough going on to fill 16 pages every week. The newsletter shows that we have a business full of amazing facts, figures and achievements. We now plan to produce a Timpson Book of Records as a new way to celebrate success.

These things give the company character and create the adrenalin that pumps around the business but they won't last long without support from the top. I want people who resist conventional managers with their conservative views and encourage the mavericks to keep breaking the rules. That's why I need leaders who are a tiny bit eccentric.

LESSONS

- Bin the paperwork
- Hand-write notes
- Praise ten times as much as you criticise
- Don't go in for mission statements
- Tell everyone everything
- Don't delegate communication
- You won't change everyone's thinking with one memo or email
- Celebrate success

Chapter 18
THE MAGIC DUST

❝It wouldn't take long for the magic dust to disappear❞ Perry Watkins

We must not be stuck in the past, but it's just as important to keep those things that have made us a great company. We must never let go of our core values and those bits of magic that have created our culture and given us the adrenalin to help the business perform far better than I could have ever expected.

We don't run our business by the book. Below are the things that I think are most important. There is nothing here about shoe repairs, key cutting, watch repairs or locksmiths. In future, we may decide to do something completely different. Some trades have disappeared from the high street; others, such as photo processing and music shops, may be in the process of disappearing. Similarly, key cutting, shoe repairs and watch repairs could disappear, although at the moment I see nothing to suggest their demise.

But, whatever business you are in, everything listed below will still apply. Treat it as a checklist and add more through your own experience. People ask for the secret of our success. There isn't one. There is just a series of good principles which add up to a load of common sense.

AIM TO BE THE BEST

Whatever you choose to do, always aim to do it better than anyone else. The market leader makes the most money. If you think that you are already the best, aim to get better. Lots of little improvements can create a five per cent increase in annual profits, which in turn leads to happiness. A five per cent fall in profit can cause misery and makes the business much more difficult to manage.

ENJOY CHANGE

Stand still at your peril. If you find change fun, you are likely to keep the business up-to-date. Think long-term: as a private business, we have a great advantage as we do not have to bother about analysts and shareholders. Think three years ahead – no one has the vision to go further – and let your imagination run riot. Then work out how to change your dreams into reality. Keep investing. Don't starve the business of cash; keep spending on refits and new machinery. Give your workforce up-to-date tools to do the job.

VISIT THE BUSINESS

However big the business becomes, keep visiting every shop – even if it's a long time between each visit. Going there and being there is the only way to really know the business. Information gained by your own eyes and ears is so much more valuable than a spreadsheet. You are not just visiting shops, you are meeting the people.

KEEP LOOKING FOR IDEAS

You don't need consultants. There are hundreds of people who work for us who know more about the business than any outsider. Our best ideas come from people on the payroll. Ideas crop up when you least expect them and in the most usual places. Most are missed by managers who are too blind to see them. Keep your eyes, ears and mind open. When you discover a half-decent idea, take a chance and give it a go. Don't worry if it doesn't succeed. You will have several failures on the way to finding a new route to success.

SHOW LEADERSHIP

Don't delegate strategy. Some people mistakenly think that upside-down management turns our business into a democracy – it doesn't. It's the chief executive's job to listen, consult, get all the facts and then make up his mind on behalf of the business. Decisions made in a committee room or at away days often finish in failure. The chief executive should show leadership – that's his job.

WIN HEARTS AND MINDS

The chief executive makes the major decisions but he doesn't tell people what to do. Implementation starts by winning people's hearts and minds. To gain support for your plan, explain what you want to do and why you want to do it. If you listen to your people in the first place, this should not be a problem. Give every decision time to sink in, as the more wholehearted the support you receive, the more successful the project will be.

WEEKLY NEWSLETTER

Our newsletter is an expensive, time-consuming project – but it works. If you are looking for the perfect magic dust, look no further. Our colleagues take it for granted but other companies can't believe that we produce 16 pages, every week, full of stories about people in our business. For 630 shops spread throughout the British Isles, it's a wonderful way to communicate.

NO SECRETS
It's simple to decide what to communicate: tell everyone everything, unless it's confidential or personal. We might be a private business but our colleagues have the right to know everything that's going on.

UPSIDE-DOWN MANAGEMENT
It has taken ten years to establish upside-down management. We are now reaping the benefits. We trust branch colleagues with the freedom to serve customers in their own way. Timpson House now provides a service to the people in our shops. It's established, everyone likes it and it really works – let's keep it that way.

AMAZE OUR CUSTOMERS
Whatever we do, wherever we do it and whatever we sell, it will always be true that the sure way to success is to amaze our customers. That should be the first line of any strategy.

OBSESSED WITH OUR PEOPLE
Two-thirds of this book is about our people, how we can look after them and the vital part they play in our success. That's about right – almost everything depends on our team.

PICK GREAT PEOPLE
Every business should put its people first. When you are recruiting and think someone might do, they won't. If you are desperately short of staff and think someone will have to do – they won't. Always pick the best, even if you have to wait some time before they come along. Our future success depends on our current recruitment. We need a business full of hard-working, honest, positive personalities. We need everyone to be A-grade. We need people who "get it".

NO BIG SHOTS

We don't want anyone who feels too big for our business. Timpson is a team; no individual should be allowed to pursue their own agenda. There are plenty of other companies where they can play that game; they are not welcome in ours.

NO HEAD OFFICE

We don't have a head office. Central administration is at Timpson House, but being at the centre does not entitle you to issue orders. No one tells our branch staff what to do. They run the business and everyone else is there to help.

NO POLITICS

I have been chief executive for 33 years. Everyone knows that James is destined to succeed me. There is no point in playing politics for the top job – or any other job. Office politics is the biggest time-waster in British business. People who can't work together as a team should try working for someone else.

NO CHEATS, NO DRONGOS

People who pinch money or falsify figures are cheats. That's gross misconduct and they are dismissed. We don't want any drongos. People who don't "get it", don't fit in – and don't create success. Every drongo should be put on a disciplinary route leading to dismissal.

GREAT PLACE TO WORK

Nothing is too good for our star performers. We already do a lot to look after our people but should be on the lookout for more. Never be tempted to save money by cutting employee benefits.

THE BONUS SCHEME

Our branch bonus scheme is a gem. It's the bonus that puts the buzz into most of our branches. Currently we pay out £5m a year in branch bonuses. That's a lot of money but we would cut it down at our peril – the people in the branches would never forgive us.

TRAINING

Our training scheme is an easy target for cost-cutting but it's our invest-ment in our major asset. Our success depends on the skill and expertise of colleagues and the quality of management. I can't think of a better way of spending money.

BE FAIR

Life is full of difficult decisions and hard choices. No one is going to agree with you all of the time but you can go through life with a clear con-science. Be fair in all your dealings. Satisfy the simple test of doing unto others what you would wish to be done to yourself.

KNOW YOUR PEOPLE

A good fashion buyer knows the weekly sales of products. We don't sell fashion, we sell a service. It's the personalities that create sales, not mer-chandise. The better you know those people, the more you know about the business. The better they know you, the more they will trust you.

LIFE-LONG EMPLOYMENT

We do not recruit managers from outside unless they are specialists. We grow our own senior team. It takes time for someone to progress from ap-prentice to regional manager, so we must promote the concept of life-long employment. We do not just promote for the sake of the business but for the individuals. Everyone has the right to reach their full potential.

SUPPORT PEOPLE IN TROUBLE

Employees give a large slice of their lives to the company. So it's only fair to show an interest in their life outside business. When they run into dif-ficulty, we should be there to help.

PRAISE

Praise is the most under-utilised tool available to management. A surprise presentation of a bottle of champagne or simply saying "well done" will spur people to greater efforts. Too many people are scared of giving praise for fear that words of congratulation will be quoted against them in a future tribunal. That's nonsense. I've never known praise to do any harm. Ninety-nine per cent of the time, praise does nothing but good.

CHARITY

We have had a company charity since 1999. Initially, it was the NSPCC. Now it's Childline. We have collected well over £1m, mostly by customers putting £1 in the box for previously no-charge jobs. Everyone wins. Employees like raising money, the charity gets more funds and customers admire the company for what we do.

CELEBRATE SUCCESS

Everyone should be proud of what we have achieved. That achievement should be recognised by finding new ways to celebrate success. Record profits, special landmarks and individual award ceremonies are excuses to have a party.

HAVE FUN

People who enjoy coming to work create a buzz that you sense when you walk in their shop or office. We want colleagues to enjoy their job. To help, do some wacky things – have an office fancy dress competition on Friday the 13th or close the office early for a game of rounders in the car park. Some managers treat business too seriously and don't realise that people who have fun make serious money.

FAMILY BUSINESS

These important elements of success would be made more difficult if we reported to institutional shareholders. The City would be suspicious of our unconventional management style. We don't fit in with their guidelines. Being a family business makes life so much easier and lets us run the business by using common sense. There is no doubt – we should keep it in the family.

LESSONS

- Aim to be the best
- Enjoy change
- Visit the business
- Keep looking for ideas
- Show leadership
- Win hearts and minds
- Weekly newsletter
- No secrets
- Upside-down management
- Amaze our customers
- Obsessed with our people
- Pick great people
- No big shots
- No head office
- No politics
- No cheats or drongos
- Great place to work
- The bonus scheme
- Training
- Be fair
- Know your people
- Life-long employment
- Support people in trouble
- Praise
- Charity
- Celebrate success
- Have fun
- Family business

Chapter 19
WHERE NEXT?

❝We must stick to the principles that created our success❞ Rosemary Whitehead

As the chairman, I enjoy a great advantage. I am released from day-to-day responsibility and have time to think ahead. Strangely, the older I get, the more my mind turns to future plans – probably years beyond my personal involvement.

The business has been a central part of my life for nearly 48 years. I want to ensure all my efforts and the work of my many colleagues has a long-term significance. It has been an interesting journey, from a publicly quoted family shoe business to a private chain of cobblers that is now the UK's biggest key cutter and watch repairer.

I could never have anticipated how things would turn out. I'm sure that the next 40 years will be just as unpredictable. But, despite that guaranteed uncertainly, we must plan ahead. (A three-year view is far enough.) What follows is a snapshot of how I see the future, as written in May 2008.

In 2000, I published my book *Dear James*. On the cover it says: "This book was conceived as a set of notes and ideas for John's son James to prepare him for taking over the company." This was a white lie; it did not start like that. The book was born following a conversation with Michael McAvoy, who has advised me on corporate communications since 1975.

In the late 1990s, following the acquisition of Automagic and introduction of several successful initiatives, we were doing well. Sales and profits had increased dramatically but I didn't think the outside world gave us the respect we deserved. "The problem is," I told Michael, "that developers don't think we're good enough for their new shopping mall. The public thinks that Timpson is still a shop that sells shoes. Jobseekers think we are an unfashionable place to work. Journalists regard cobblers as a bit of a joke. Timpson is much better than that. I am proud of lots of things that we do. It's about time we improved our image."

Michael's answer was simple: get someone to write a book about the story of Timpson and how its success had been created. I understood what he was saying but I didn't want anyone else to write the book. If it was to be written, I would write it myself. I had one worry. A book about success under my management could be seen as arrogant. I filled it with stories of failure as well as success and wrote it in the context of a blueprint for James – hence the title *Dear James*.

As a PR exercise, it worked. At the book launch, I met someone from the DTI who suggested that we should enter into a survey, conducted in conjunction with the *Sunday Times*. A few months later, when the first "Best Place to Work" survey was published, we were third out of a list of 50. Next year, the list was extended to 100 companies; we were fourth. We did just as well in a rival *Financial Times* survey, again coming in the top ten. We had been noticed. As a result, I wrote a few contributions for the *Sunday Times* and started to write my monthly column in the magazine *Real Business*. James and I received requests to speak at business conferences, where delegates seemed intrigued by our upside-down management style.

Although a few people think I still run shoe shops, many more see Timpson as a great company to work for. The publicity has improved our recruitment, although we still get turned down by some landlords who think that shoe repairers are noisy, smelly, dirty and unwelcome in their new development.

The *Sunday Times* list was good to us but we haven't featured since 2005. We stopped entering for several good reasons. The list was starting to lack authority. It was hijacked by PR agencies, lawyers and consultants. Professional companies started to dominate the list, putting blue-collar high street workers such as us at a disadvantage. There was a suspicion of cheating; the results relied heavily on responses to a detailed employee survey. Some companies massaged the findings. One, it was rumoured, gathered their employers together and supervised the box ticking to ensure the right result. We were not happy when the *Sunday Times* introduced an entry fee. It didn't feel right to have to pay to be on the list. But the main reason we stopped entering was more fundamental. The *Sunday Times* required a minimum response of 40 per cent to their employee survey. We struggled to reach that level; our people don't like filling in forms. To feature in a list of great places to work, we were asking employees to do something they detested.

Back to *Dear James*. Those who know James well realise that he has a mind of his own. It is a determination inherited from his mother. I can't be sure how much of *Dear James* he took on board, but we very much enjoy working together. Few families will have a stronger business partnership. Some friends thought that *Dear James* was the announcement of my retirement. They asked me whether I still had a role in the business.

I practise upside-down management. I am responsible for strategy and communication; James runs the day-to-day business. Although I fit in golf, tennis, real tennis, horse-racing and plenty of holidays, the majority of my time is spent with the business. I still know all our shops and visit them regularly. I never got hooked on the TV soaps – the business is my *Coronation Street*, *EastEnders* and *Neighbours* rolled into one. To do my job, I need to know the business in detail.

When I met Ian Siddall, after UBS had bought Minit, he told me that he was an expert at running family businesses properly. He put in "professional management". Even these days, I am asked whether I have brought in professional management. One of our greatest assets is our 100 per cent ownership – but it only works if the owners run the business. If James hadn't wanted to join the company and nobody else in the family had the talent and dedication to run it, I would probably be planning to sell up. But such thoughts could not be further from my mind. I won't sell a single share.

On my 64th birthday, I received a "grumpy old man" DVD and several pointed questions about my status. "Are you retired?" "Does your son do it all now?" "What's your exit?" These days everyone assumes there is an exit. Self-made entrepreneurs float at a dizzy p/e ratio and, after a year working for institutional shareholders, escape to their yacht and join the jet set. Computer whizzkids cash in before the technology moves on, while their venture capitalist backers always have an exit.

My father taught me to take a different view: the ownership of shares gives you the responsibility to care for a business and its people. Running a family business is a privilege, providing as much joy from creating success as you derive from the dividends.

I regularly receive junk mail, promising me ways to save tax and how to turn my death into a huge benefit for the family. But I don't want to live in Jersey or give the company to Alex and buy her a house in Monaco.

My great-grandfather set up a business that lasted for more than 100 years. Eventually, I lived through a family feud that led to a takeover and ended 108 years of family ownership. The feud brought a surprising outcome. At a stroke, uncles, nieces and second cousins ceased to be shareholders. Two buyouts and a trade sale later, the business was back in family hands – but this time I was the only shareholder.

In this guise, we haven't been going much more than 20 years, so there is still a long way to go. I have some tips designed to keep our independence.

Rule 1: Do not sell shares in the company outside the family.
Rule 2: Keep the business up-to-date and invest in the future.
Rule 3: Look after the people who work in the business.
Rule 4: Let only talented family members enter the boardroom.
Rule 5: Have two non-executive directors from outside the family.
Rule 6: Host a family party every year to tell everyone what's going on in the business.
Rule 7: If you discover that you are yesterday's business and see no future, ignore Rule 1.
Rule 8: If you run out of family talent, sell the business – preferably to the management team.

I have avoided Tony Blair's mistake of naming the day of my departure, but all this retirement talk made me wonder whether I had outlived my welcome. Should I, like Shane Warne, retire at the top?

My self-esteem was restored by the birthday present I received from James. It was an expensive briefcase with a ten-year guarantee. Bolstered by that vote of confidence, I plan to hang on until the bitter end – in the hope that Alex and I have produced enough descendants with the flair to develop the business but not so many that they fight amongst themselves and destroy their inheritance. In the meantime, I intend to develop a company worth squabbling over.

We are lucky. James has the talent and determination the business needs. James and I make a good team. Father-and-son relationships do not always create business success but, for us, despite a healthy competitive tension when it comes to creating new ideas, we find it works well.

When I wrote *Dear James*, our turnover was £45m and profit was £2.2m. Seven years later, sales are £105m and profits have risen to £12.5m. James is aiming for a lot more. As he pointed out, some Chelsea players are paid £140,000 per week, so our profit only equates to two footballers.

The Minit acquisition has been the main driver of our recent improvement. But it's not the only reason. Watch repair turnover has reached £12m from a standing start – a tangible return from our major investment in training. The biggest change in the past seven years has been our people. I thought they were good but now they are much better, showing the benefit of recruiting personalities and having a proper apprentice scheme. We have turned those personalities into craftsmen, with many now running shops with large turnovers. We have a much stronger management team, particularly in the field where our area teams are completely home-grown. We have also brought in a few professional managers, such as finance director Paresh Majithia; finance controller Helen Thompson; controller of buying Sally Eve; and Paul Churchill in IT. It hasn't taken them long to learn about upside-down management and a culture dominated by common sense.

With a strong home-grown area structure, we have the capability to take on many more shops. We are opening 35 new branches each year but, with an estimated saturation point of 900, there are still more than 300 to open, plus the replacements to improve our portfolio.

We have had the exceptional recent benefit of stiletto heels. They won't stay in fashion much longer and shoe repair turnover will suffer. We will gain extra sales from other services such as watch repairs, jewellery repairs, dry cleaning and photo ID. But the five per cent like-for-like increases that we have enjoyed for several years will be much tougher to achieve.

Our profit improvement has generated cash. It's been enough to pay off past leasing and borrowings and, until the next major acquisition, our bank account should be permanently in credit.

Despite this strong position, we still listen to our bank manager. He often talks about a three-legged stool, liking businesses that have several sources of profit. Diversification helps spread the risk.

Our core high street service shops continue to be a great business but the potential is limited. We have firmly decided not to trade outside the British Isles: this is a people business that needs hands-on management. I wouldn't be comfortable running shops in another culture and a different language. So, heeding the advice of our bank manager, we are growing some extra legs that have arrived more by chance than by careful planning.

In 1985, when our shoe retail and repair business were both struggling, we opened a shop in Altrincham called "Security Now". It sold key-cutting, locksmith work and alarm systems. It was successful enough to open two more shops in Wilmslow and Stockport, but it never made the money we hoped for. In 1989 we closed Security Now and forgot about diversification.

In 1997 two locksmiths, Darren Pemberton and Brent Hulme, came to see me. They had used their redundancy money to start their own business in Oldham Road, Manchester. Their business was a success but they lacked the support of a head office. They needed finance to expand. We bought the business and, true to their word, Darren and Brent did so well that we acquired another locksmith in Preston, run by Mick Singleton. Darren, Mick and Brent showed us that Timpson Locksmiths could become a big business. We now have 25 vans, a sales team, and a call centre with turnover growing rapidly. We are learning something new about this brand-new world every day. The dream of a national locksmith service is fast becoming a reality.

In 1989 we got into the house sign business because we bought a computer engraver. This big machine put us at the leading edge of engraving technology, but we didn't know what to do with it. At first, we used it to engrave trophies, tankards and gifts but we soon discovered a demand for signs. Enthused by the potential, I spent three days taking pictures of every sign I could find. I surreptitiously snapped signs outside dentists, physiotherapists, small lawyers and accountants. I took pictures of memorial plaques, "Beware of the Dog" signs, and "Rose Cottage" signs. The time spent in graveyards, high streets and suburbs produced a big display in ten shops. We discovered the bestsellers were house signs. We filled a pilaster board with the most popular signs and displayed it outside every shop – house sign sales took off.

But I wasn't happy. Our signs were engraved, but the nation's most popular ones were cast in brass. We found the biggest supplier of cast signs, the House Nameplate Company (HNP) based outside Wrexham. Despite a higher retail price and much slower delivery time, HNP signs sold well. We didn't like their margins but it still made us money. Our business with HNP grew; we became their third largest customer after B&Q and Homebase. Andy Jones and Guy Tyrell, the owners of HNP, attended our 2001 suppliers' lunch. Before leaving, Guy asked me whether I would be interested in buying their company. Our negotiations didn't reach a conclusion until 2004, when HNP joined the Timpson Group.

The first 18 months were difficult. DIY retailers were suffering a severe slump and the HNP range needed a facelift. For two years, we saw little return on our investment. Sales suffered at Homebase. Wyevale moved to another supplier. The only sales increase came from the extra HNP signs displayed in our own shops. In 2007, we spent £500,000 launching a new range in B&Q, doubling their turnover of house signs. The B&Q team recognised we had the ability to develop new products and deliver on time, so they gave us more floor space in their stores. HNP is now poised to become a significant supplier to the DIY trade and is growing into a permanent future leg of our business.

It took us some time to realise the biggest problem that diversification brings. It is fashionable to go plural but few people can run more than one company at once. We were tempted to think that, because we run a successful shoe repair business, we could turn our hand to locksmithing and house signs at the same time. We couldn't. The core business needed too much of our attention, because it made so much of our profit.

I didn't solve this problem; it was solved by chance. My niece, Tina Smith, came to see me just after Christmas 2005. At the time, she was managing director of Westbury Homes in the north-west and responsible for a £23m annual profit. But she had a problem. Westbury was being taken over by Persimmon and her future was insecure. We talked through the options: stay with Persimmon, set up on her own, or work for a venture capitalist. At a second meeting a fortnight later, we talked of another idea. By the end of February, Tina had joined us as managing director, new business, with responsibility for the locksmiths and HNP. Her single-minded interest in making our new ventures successful has made a massive difference. You can't diversify unless you are willing to delegate.

Tina is also responsible for another quirky Timpson business that has proved to be a surprising source of profit: Keys Direct. It supplies lockers and keys to large organisations whose staff change into uniforms at work. The keys are cut according to a computer database back at Wythenshawe. Like the rest of Timpson, the success of Keys Direct depends on our people – led in this case by Clive Stirling, who was James's sales manager when he was gaining work experience in the North East with Apparelmaster, part of Johnson the Cleaners.

The fifth leg of our three-legged stool has the strangest origin of all. In April 2003, Alex persuaded me to buy a cottage in Anglesey. "It's fantastic," said Alex, after we finished the major extension, "but there is one problem." My heart sank. There were no decent restaurants. (Alex hates cooking, so dining out is very important.) "But I have a solution," she continued. "Buy the pub. It's only 400 yards away. With a good chef, we would have wonderful food on the doorstep and they could deliver to our cottage."

I ignored this bizarre suggestion. Six months later, on holiday in the Caribbean, I received an email from James: the owners of the White Eagle wanted to convert the pub into flats and the residents had organised a protest meeting. That was enough for Alex. On our return, I sent a written offer that was accepted two days later. Before exchanging contracts, we attended a six hour licensees' course – the first exam either of us had taken in more than 40 years.

The day before completion, Alex installed Kirsty and Stuart as managers and Terry as chef. "This will be fun," she said, before going to bed in our cottage, happy with her latest acquisition.

Stuart rang at 7am the next morning. "It's a nightmare," he started. "This is the worst pub I have ever seen."

We called on our way to Llangefni Magistrate's Court and immediately saw why Stuart was upset. The pub was filthy. The freezer was full of fast food. The only fresh ingredients were three tomatoes and lots of limp lettuce. There were plastic flowers inside and no flowers in the tubs outside. The till didn't work and sewage was seeping into the car park.

As a chairman, I avoid day-to-day problems but Alex rose to the occasion. She bought two vacuum cleaners, three mops, a bucket and dollops of disinfectant so the White Eagle clean-up could begin.

As we approached the Magistrate's Court, she turned on me. "What contribution are you making?" she asked. I decided it was time to involve Timpson in the equation.

I rang Steve Marsh, our warehouse manager, who deals with difficult problems all the time. "Are you anywhere near Anglesey?" I asked.

Steve fixed the septic tank and got to work on other nasty problems such as the payroll payments and supplier issues. Alex adopted Gordon Ramsey's recipe for success without the f-words – a simple menu with fresh, local produce. The customers were pleased and sales took off.

I basked in her reflected glory, spreading the news about our crazy venture and the award of our licensee certificate. I found that, by becoming a publican, I attracted many more friends and most have plenty of tips on how to run a pub.

Within a month Alex had flowers in the hanging baskets, good quality loo paper and loads of compliments about the food. Then we hit a major problem. Stuart and Kirsty decided to leave. The agency sent a couple with lots of qualifications but no charisma. The buzz went from the pub and turnover started to drop. Thankfully, three weeks later, Steve persuaded Stuart and Kirsty to come back. Then Alex got stuck into her development plan.

"No point in half measures," she said. "If we alter the pub we must do it properly." I expected to spend £400,000 but, having seen Alex's plans, the budget rose to £1.2m.

A lot of entrepreneurs own restaurants and pubs. Much to my surprise, The White Eagle is not an albatross. I never expected this madcap scheme to make much business sense but, even before the alterations, trade was growing by 50 per cent and we were making a profit. Alex's refit was so extensive that she knocked most of the pub down. We were closed for more than eight months. When we re-opened, I discovered she had doubled the number of tables, dramatically improved the décor and installed a state-of-the-art kitchen. She had even improved the view and achieved sales way beyond my expectation. It is amazing to think that it all started as a take-away service for Alex.

I now worry that Alex will want a chain of pubs. I hope that I have persuaded her that it owes its success to being unique. "There can only be one White Eagle," I told her.

A lot has changed in the world outside Timpson. Companies now concentrate on being compliant, following guidelines written to help management teams who are frightened to break the rules. The biggest shift is in employment law, drafted to protect the poorest performers. They don't want us to discriminate against drongos.

Actuaries, accountants and the government, in an orgy of prudence, caused a large slice of industry to abandon final salary pension schemes. The Pensions Regulator created a stampede towards money purchase funding or no funding at all, making most pensioners worse off in an attempt to shelter the few victims of those schemes that go bust.

Health and safety has become a universal excuse for unnecessary expenditure and lack of initiative, measured by red tape and maintained by steering committees. Now we are seeing the growth of social responsibility, with particular reference to the environment. Soon the world's most recognised KPI will be a carbon footprint instead of a balance sheet.

Too many people think that you can create success by following a set of rules. In my experience, best practice is no substitute for common sense.

LISTEN

Serve some customers

Admit your mistakes

Don't walk past a problem

Don't stay behind your desk

Our first management book, *How to be a Great Boss*, explains upside-down management in lots of pictures and very few words.

How to pick great people

The Timpson Way

How to create more time

The Timpson Way

How to increase your bonus

The Timpson Way

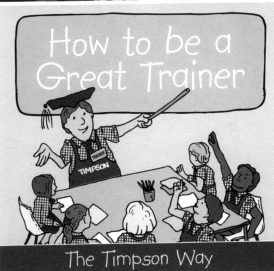

The Timpson Way

How to be a great employee

The Timpson Way

How to create a great place to work

The Timpson Way

How to be a great BIG BOSS

Using Controversial Common Sense

How to make shopping fun

The Timpson Way

How to avoid an Employment Tribunal

The Timpson Way

Above: Our library of books provides the fundamental material for our management training scheme. More than 5,000 copies have been bought by other businesses from the Timpson website.

Opposite: Our training manuals, too, use pictures rather than words.

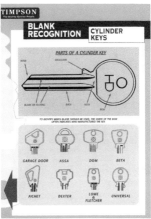

BLANK RECOGNITION — CYLINDER KEYS

PARTS OF A CYLINDER KEY

TO IDENTIFY WHICH BLANK SHOULD BE USED, THE SHAPE OF THE BOW OFTEN INDICATES WHO MANUFACTURED THE KEY

GARAGE DOOR · ASSA · DOM · BETA
FICHET · DEXTER · LOWE & FLETCHER · UNIVERSAL

CUTTING MORTICE KEYS — JAKEY MK2

LEVER CUTS

KEYS TO CODE

WHAT MAKES A LOCK WORK

MORTICE

TIMPSON
The Quality Service People
GUIDE TO KEY CUTTING

APPRENTICESHIP MANUAL

TIMPSON
The Quality Service People
GUIDE TO ENGRAVING

MANAGER

TIMPSON
The Quality Service People
WATCH REPAIR MANUAL

TIMPSON
The Quality Service People
THE AREA MANAGER'S GUIDE

TIMPSON
The Quality Service People
GUIDE TO EXPERT SHOE REPAIRS

Above: *The Timpson Weekly News* keeps everyone up-to-date with the company headlines. The inside pages are mainly about people.

Opposite: Our upside-down management chart.

CUSTOMERS

THE BRANCH STAFF

TRUSTED WITH CONTROL

TIMPSON HOUSE   **AREA TEAM**   **WORKSHOPS**

PROVIDES HELP AND SUPPORT

SENIOR MANAGEMENT

PROVIDES HELP AND SUPPORT

CHAIRMAN

PROVIDES HELP AND SUPPORT

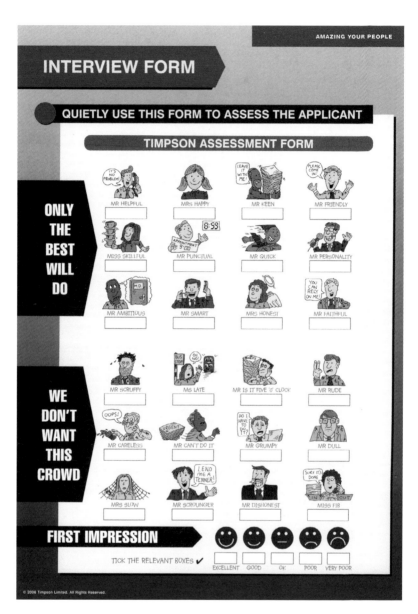

Above: Our interview form.

Opposite top: This notice is displayed in every branch.
Opposite middle: Our customer care training chart.
Opposite bottom: "Free Jobs" have raised over £1.5m for ChildLine.

Customer Challenge

Most customers are a miserable bunch

Make them smile!

Try and create enough fun to make them smile

TIMPSON
The Quality Service People

Small Jobs!
Holes in Belts
Glueing & Stitching

Donate £1 to ChildLine and we will DOUBLE IT!

ChildLine
0800 1111

Small Jobs for ChildLine

ChildLine
0800 1111

203

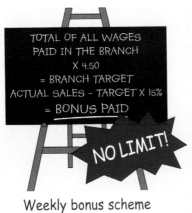

Weekly bonus scheme

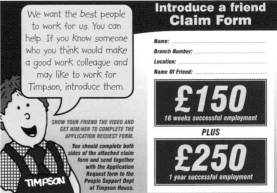

Three ideas that really work.

Top left: How the bonus scheme works. It puts a buzz into all our shops.

Top right: We check the cash everyday against the same day last year.

Bottom: Our introduce-a-friend scheme brings in 45 per cent of our new recruits.

Chapter 20
IN CONCLUSION

Some people think I'm an eccentric optimist. At heart, though, I'm paranoid. I share the optimism of the people I spoke to on my tour around the country with my A4 pad. That's because the evidence is clear: our management style works, our culture has created success and has, in the process, produced a relatively stress-free environment that allows people to enjoy their job.

But I am worried. How long will it last? So many well-known names have disappeared from the high street. Even the most successful companies can hit hard times if management loses the plot. My worries are not due to a further decline in shoe repairs or a move away from traditional keys to something we can't cut. I fear future generations will forget how we created our success and return to traditional methods led by a professional manager. If our company fell into the hands of a leader that didn't get it, all the achievements over the past 20 years could be undone in a matter of months.

Writing this book has taught me a lot about our colleagues. I have been amazed at their loyalty and how much they enjoy success. I won't forget the time I was told, "when I came back to work at Timpson, I felt I was coming home". Our people have greater insight into what makes a difference than I had expected.

To harness their views and keep us in touch with the magic dust, we have created the Timpson Culture Club. It's a small group of seven of us who will disappear for a meeting twice a year to monitor the vital elements of our management style and promote new ways to make the company even better.

The club members are chosen from all parts of the business. Selection is not based on seniority (apart from the permanent post of James as chairman and myself as president). All members know the business well enough to demonstrate they have "got it". The club has no executive authority but will report directly to the board and discuss every major change before it is implemented.

Each member will keep a close eye on some important parts of our culture – the benefits such as the holiday homes, the truth behind our management style and the openness of our communications. It's no coincidence that two of the members of our Culture Club played such a big part in supplying material for this book. They helped me discover the vital ingredients behind our success. If the club fulfils its purpose, it will protect the things – great and small – that make a big difference.

Throughout this book, I recognise the vital part played by Timpson colleagues. But we will always need a leader. The leader must want to grow the business by being the best at what we do, know how to pick personalities and recognise the importance of looking after them. It can be done. My great-grandfather started a company that lasted for over 100 years. We have only just passed 20 years of independence. There is a long way to go.

Louise Appleby
69

Darren Brown
73-8, 117, 173 (pic)

Paul Churchill
192

Mike Donoghue
26, 105, 120

Brian Armstrong
97

Richard (Dick)
Bujnicki
66, 126 (pic)

Gail Cobb
57

Gareth Drewe
81

Andy Ball
66

Kerry Burke
22

Ray Cooley
22

James Durno
62

Alex Barrett
23, 62, 78-81,
91 (pic), 159

Alan Chatterton
57

Jo Cooper
88

Chris Edwards
23

Ricky Bickell
23

Simon Childs
81, 112 (pic)

Fran Donaghy
48, 62

Glenn Edwards
26, 144

Brian Elliott
97

Geoff Goodfellow
26

Winston Harris
23

Brent Hulme
192

Sally Eve
192

Jim Gow
78

Fred Harrison
75

Osman Isaaq
87

Michael Frank
56

Kit Green
27, 57, 85-6, 168 (pic)

Chris Hart
26

Jim Jardine
23

Ian Gallagher
66-7

Ashley Griffiths
109

Les Hart
26

Adrian Jennison
86

Arnaud Gois
108

Peter Harris
26, 58, 119 (pic), 160

Sid Hubbard
57

Andy Jones
193

Karina Kenna
68-70, 84 (pic)

Paresh Majithia
72-3, 129 (pic)

Steve Melville
73

Ralph O'Brien
49

Divna Kisic
86

Jim Malcolm
22

Alan Milne
62

Bill O'Dell
23

Brian Lowe
93

Steve Marsh
195

Rab Mitchell
88

PJ O'Sullivan
86, 104

Hayley McGinley
109

Paul Masters
54, 65, 156 (pic)

Paul Myatt
22, 56

Darren Pemberton
192

Alan Madden
23

Barbara Mead
59-61, 100 (pic)

Bob Northover
104

Bill Platt
96

Rosemary
Whitehead
82, 187 (pic)

Stewart Williams
86

Keith Winter
70

Philip Whitmore
73

Andy Willingham
53

INDEX